1- HOW TO USE THIS	...1
2- MY PORTFOLIO	11
3- PERSONAL	19
4- REGULATION	9
5- KNOWLEDGE	37
6- POLICIES	73
7- FULL INDEX	141
8- ANNUAL DECLARATION	145

My Portfolio:
A record of your learning experiences and training sessions

Personal Development:
Record how your skills have developed during the year

Regulations and Safe Care:
Learn the legal terms and our legal requirements

Knowledge & Training:
A quick recap and self-assessment of training and knowledge

Policies:
Key policies necessary for your job

Full Index:
Index to help you find things quickly

Annual Declaration:
Your annual certificate of completion

Your Achievement Level

Each star means an achievement for you. If you are unsure about something, asking for help and making sure you get it are achievements because it shows a responsible attitude.

Your level of completion

Achievement

	Started	Section read	Asked for help	Got the help	Completed
	1	2	3	4	5
1. How to use this book	☆	☆	☆	☆	★
2. My portfolio	☆	☆	☆	☆	★
3. Personal development	☆	☆	☆	☆	★
4. Regulations and safe care	☆	☆	☆	☆	★
5. Knowledge & training record	☆	☆	☆	☆	★
6. Policies	☆	☆	☆	☆	★
8. Annual Declaration	☆	☆	☆	☆	★

What it will look like when you've completed a section

Completed, no help was needed
Read it, but I need help on some things
Got the help now, I'm all done
Completed, ready to sign off

1- How to use this book

For Staff
This is your personal record of your activity and Professional Development for the entire year, keep it with you at all times during work so you can easily record things as they happen.

If your employer got this for you, it would belong to them. You should always ask for permission before you take it home and be clear what you should do with it if you ever leave the job.

For Managers
Ensure everyone is clear about safe keeping and day to day control over this Passport. Try to delegate management of this task to a suitable member of staff, it will empower them and make them feel valued as they assume responsibility. Staff respond more positively if a fellow team member is looking after this, and it also helps reduce your own workload.

This Passport is a formal record and is part of an employee's personnel file, so ensure everyone is clear about ownership and retention at the end of an employment.
You will find more guidance and tips on best practice and how to use this in Group training at everythingCQC.com

© everythingCQC.com All rights reserved
Produced by everythingCQC.com under licence from X-Genics Limited and MaDiHC Limited

1.1- It's your personal Passport

Personalise the Passport cover before you start working on it.

Make it yours
Stick your photo on the cover, write your name and the organisation name. Add the address in case it gets lost outside the work place, so people know where to return it.

When did you last read this
The calendar grid on the cover is your quick record of when you last read this Passport. Tick the month box every time you read this.

At the end of the year
When you are finished with this Passport, complete the Annual Review on the inside back cover. In most cases this will be countersigned by the manager to certify your completion and will be part of your training and development record.

Keep it safe
Keep this Passport safe. It is easy to replace if you lose it, but it means you might have to do your work all over again.

1.2- Getting Started

Familiarise yourself with this book. This is easy, just look through the book very quickly so you can see where everything is.
There is a brief description at the beginning of each section to help you understand what it is for.

Be honest
1. If you are not confident about something, be honest about it, you can come back later to show you have improved.
2. It is OK to not know something then ask someone and then come back to say that you now understand
3. If you say you're good even though you're not, no one will know that you need help.
4. This is your chance to tell your supervisor that you need more help

Asking for help
1. If you don't understand something, you can mark it in the book by underlining it or drawing a circle around it.
2. Then speak to a colleague, your supervisor or manager who can explain this. Once you understand it better, you can sign off the section as completed.
3. You will be using this throughout the year and can record improvements as often as you want.

1.3- You Can Write in This Book

This book is like your diary, don't be afraid of writing in it and making notes on the pages.

Who cares if it gets messy, it shows that you are really using it and next year you'll get a new book anyway.

1.1- Being Professional

Skills and competency
Your skills and ability to work well make you a valued member of your team.
- Keep up to date with training and skills
- Try to improve your work
- People like working with skilled colleagues
- The better you are at your job, the more valued you become

Personal Conduct
Always maintain a high standard of conduct and work performance by: *What's this?*
- Observing rules, regulations and policies
- Treating colleagues (with courtesy and respect)
- Treating Service Users and visitors in a professional manner
- Working safely

Remember that the way you act with others reflects on our image as a team.

Accepting Gifts
People often like to thank us by giving gifts. This puts you in a difficult situation as others may see this as a bribe or people might then expect you to do favours in return.

To avoid this, whenever gifts are offered by anyone at all, the safest option is to refuse to take these in a polite way. If in doubt, ask your Manager for help. If anyone accepts bribes, they could be prosecuted under The Bribery Act.

Must remember this for staff meeting ......

1.4- Rate Your Confidence on Topics

1. Read each topic, it should only take a couple of minutes
2. If you're unsure about a word or a paragraph, underline it or draw a circle around it to remind yourself
3. Ask a colleague, your supervisor or manager about the things that were not clear
4. If a topic doesn't apply to you, you can cross it out

Giving a temporary low rating looks like this:

1	2	3	4	5
☐	☐	✓	☐	☐

Rate your confidence on this topic out of 5

You can rate it as many times as you like

1. A low rating is not like getting bad marks in an exam. It shows your supervisor that they need to explain things a little better
2. If you had trouble understanding something, then someone else probably had the same trouble and your supervisor needs to know

Rating it again when it becomes clearer will look like this:

1	2	3	4	5
☐	☐	✓	☐	✓

Rate your confidence on this topic out of 5

What this will show

1. You're honest when you don't understand
2. You're not afraid to ask and learn
3. You want to improve your knowledge

1.5- Different Ways of Working

Who keeps this book?
There are different ways of doing this
1. The manager keeps this book so that all books are together and kept safe. It will be given to you when you need to work on it and must be returned to them so they know the task is completed and can help you with anything you did not understand.
2. You keep the book all the time, and it will be your duty to make sure it is kept safe and you don't lose it.

Individual learning
You will be assigned one or more topics to read by your manager. Most topics take just a few minutes to read. If something is not clear, ask as soon as possible, then you can sign off the topic as completed.

Team workshops
You can work in a team to learn about the topics together and have a discussion about how this applies in your daily work. This can be done at proper staff meetings or even during your coffee break if you find this easier.

Group Training
You might be invited to group meetings where many others might be attending from other organisations. Everyone will have their own book, so you can discuss this and work through the topics in small workshops.

1.6- You can take it anywhere

You can work on your own or get face-to-face training

Use it at staff meetings or have group discussions

Even lectures and workshops can be organised around this passport

Organise two boxes at work.
- Label one as "All OK" and one as "Need help"

- Once help is provided, staff re-rate the topic, and the book goes in the "All OK" box, ready for filing away.
- So easy to manage, everyone knows exactly what to do.

1.7- What if ?

What if you come across some of these issues.

This doesn't apply to me
If you come across a topic that doesn't apply to you, read it anyway, it adds to your knowledge. You can also cross it out to show you decided it doesn't apply to you.

I know more than this
The topics are just a summary and basic knowledge. If you come across topics where you know more, and you think others will benefit from your knowledge, then this is a great opportunity to tell your manager or talk about this with your colleagues or at meetings. It is important that we learn from each other's experience.

Something is missing
You might see something here that your organisation has missed or the other way around where you think your team does more than what this Passport says.

Treat this as an opportunity to start a conversation about this topic with your colleagues, your manager and your team. Others may not have spotted this, and once again it's an opportunity for people to learn from each other.

1.8- First Time Use

This book helps you record how you refresh and keep up to date with the essential knowledge and training you will have received already. You must always have an induction before you start work with a new employer

What is an induction
When you first join an organisation, your Supervisor or Manager will want to make sure that you know the rules and procedures to be followed, the people you will work with, all the contact numbers and how the organisation works. This is called an induction, and your introduction to the organisation.

At this induction, your supervisor will also make sure you have all the basic skills, training and personal equipment so that you can carry out all your tasks properly.

Can I skip inductions
You should never skip inductions, especially as some tasks, such as manual handling of patients or using lifts and other equipment, need to be done at a face-to-face training session so you can be shown how to do this.

If you already know things, then use the induction as a chance to practice your skills and ask questions about your tasks.

2- My Portfolio

Keep a record of your experiences and learning

1. Positive experiences you are proud of
2. Suggestions for improvements
3. Things you learned that have made you better at your job
4. Log your staff training sessions
5. Log any external training you received during the year

What you will achieve

1. You will have a diary of learning and experiences for the year with everything in one place.

2. You will be well organised whenever you need to speak to your manager about what you have achieved and how things are going in your job.

3. Everything you record here will count towards your professional development.

2.2- My Positive Experiences

My personal achievements/Positive things/Things I did this year that I'm proud of

What happened	How I solved it
Date ____/____/____	
Date ____/____/____	
Date ____/____/____	
Date ____/____/____	
Date ____/____/____	

2.3- My Suggestions for Improvement

Suggest improvements that will improve the organisation or the way we provide services

Subject	Your suggestion
Date ___/___/___	
Date ___/___/___	
Date ___/___/___	
Date ___/___/___	
Date ___/___/___	

2.4- Staff Training Record

Personal training and staff meeting training that you received at work

Date	Subject	Give it a star rating
		☆☆☆☆☆
		☆☆☆☆☆
		☆☆☆☆☆
		☆☆☆☆☆
		☆☆☆☆☆
		☆☆☆☆☆
		☆☆☆☆☆
		☆☆☆☆☆
		☆☆☆☆☆
		☆☆☆☆☆
		☆☆☆☆☆
		☆☆☆☆☆
		☆☆☆☆☆
		☆☆☆☆☆

2.5- Staff Training Record

Personal training and staff meeting training that you received at work

Date	Subject	Give it a star rating
		☆☆☆☆☆
		☆☆☆☆☆
		☆☆☆☆☆
		☆☆☆☆☆
		☆☆☆☆☆
		☆☆☆☆☆
		☆☆☆☆☆
		☆☆☆☆☆
		☆☆☆☆☆
		☆☆☆☆☆
		☆☆☆☆☆
		☆☆☆☆☆
		☆☆☆☆☆
		☆☆☆☆☆

2.6- External Courses and Online Training

If you went to courses or seminars you can record it here

Date	Subject	Give it a star rating
		☆☆☆☆☆
		☆☆☆☆☆
		☆☆☆☆☆
		☆☆☆☆☆
		☆☆☆☆☆
		☆☆☆☆☆
		☆☆☆☆☆
		☆☆☆☆☆
		☆☆☆☆☆
		☆☆☆☆☆
		☆☆☆☆☆
		☆☆☆☆☆
		☆☆☆☆☆
		☆☆☆☆☆

Training and Courses - Things I need help on

Date / Page	Note of what you need help on (Tick as 'Done' when you've got the help)	Done
		☐
		☐
		☐
		☐
		☐
		☐
		☐
		☐
Speak to your manager or supervisor to get help on the topic		

3- Personal Development

This section is a quick self-assessment of your abilities and how you have progressed through the year.

What you have to do: -
1. Rate your knowledge and confidence when you first start
2. Change this whenever you like
3. Record your improvements during the year
4. Ask for help if you need

How to use this: -
1. Do a quick review at the start
2. Don't worry about leaving blanks if you are not sure
3. It doesn't matter how you rate yourself right now
4. You can revisit and change this as many times as you want

This will form a part of your staff appraisal and help you achieve improvements.

3.1- About Me

Performance

How do you rate yourself?

1	2	3	4	5

- I understand my job description
- My timekeeping
- My personal appearance
- My professional ability
- My reliability
- I like to improve myself
- I accept all tasks given to me
- My Sickness record
- My commitment to work
- I can work under pressure

Health and Safety

How do you rate yourself?

1	2	3	4	5

- Awareness of own safety requirements
- Knowledge of Health and Safety Policy
- I know what is COSHH/RIDDOR
- Knowledge of workplace risk issues

3.2 - Working with Others

Working in a Team

How do you rate yourself?

1	2	3	4	5

Can work well in a team ☐ ☐ ☐ ☐ ☐
Relationship with other team members ☐ ☐ ☐ ☐ ☐
Contributes at meetings ☐ ☐ ☐ ☐ ☐
Can communicate with other health professionals ☐ ☐ ☐ ☐ ☐

Working with Service Users

How do you rate yourself?

1	2	3	4	5

Takes time to listen to Service Users ☐ ☐ ☐ ☐ ☐
Can communicate with Service Users ☐ ☐ ☐ ☐ ☐
Is sympathetic towards people ☐ ☐ ☐ ☐ ☐
Ability to handle difficult people ☐ ☐ ☐ ☐ ☐
Understands confidentiality ☐ ☐ ☐ ☐ ☐

3.3- Approach to Work

How you Work

How do you rate yourself?

	1	2	3	4	5
Keeps clear and accurate records	☐	☐	☐	☐	☐
Checks own performance	☐	☐	☐	☐	☐
Able to accept constructive criticism	☐	☐	☐	☐	☐
Able to give constructive criticism	☐	☐	☐	☐	☐
Can be assertive when needed	☐	☐	☐	☐	☐

3.4 - Office Admin – Records and Filing

Storing Information

How do you rate yourself?

1	2	3	4	5

	1	2	3	4	5
Able to perform care record searches	☐	☐	☐	☐	☐
Understands electronic filing systems	☐	☐	☐	☐	☐
Understands paper filing systems	☐	☐	☐	☐	☐
Keeps documents safe and secure	☐	☐	☐	☐	☐
Understands document confidentiality	☐	☐	☐	☐	☐
Keeps files and documents completed	☐	☐	☐	☐	☐

Filing Systems

How do you rate yourself?

	1	2	3	4	5
Understanding these filing systems:	☐	☐	☐	☐	☐
Manual or paper based	☐	☐	☐	☐	☐
Computerised records	☐	☐	☐	☐	☐
Alphabetical filing	☐	☐	☐	☐	☐
Numerical filing	☐	☐	☐	☐	☐
Alphanumeric filing	☐	☐	☐	☐	☐

3.5 - Office Admin – communications

Receive and Send Information

How do you rate yourself?

1	2	3	4	5

Telephone systems
- Ability to take messages ☐ ☐ ☐ ☐ ☐
- Knowledge of telephone systems ☐ ☐ ☐ ☐ ☐

Fax machine:
- Using fax machine ☐ ☐ ☐ ☐ ☐
- Fax routing information ☐ ☐ ☐ ☐ ☐

E-Mail systems:
- Sending information ☐ ☐ ☐ ☐ ☐
- Receiving information ☐ ☐ ☐ ☐ ☐
- Attaching files ☐ ☐ ☐ ☐ ☐
- Text formatting ☐ ☐ ☐ ☐ ☐
- Email security ☐ ☐ ☐ ☐ ☐

Scanning documents ☐ ☐ ☐ ☐ ☐

3.6 - Organisation Skills

Personal Organisation

How do you rate yourself?

1	2	3	4	5

- Ability to prioritise own workload
- Time management
- Uses own initiative
- Ordering of resources
- Ability to abide by rules and procedures

Management Skills

How do you rate yourself?

1	2	3	4	5

- Leading a team
- Motivating people
- Managing quality assurance
- Managing and supervising people

3.7- Healthcare Office Skills

Correspondence

How do you rate yourself?

1	2	3	4	5

Written communication ☐ ☐ ☐ ☐ ☐
Layout of documents ☐ ☐ ☐ ☐ ☐
Using different types of correspondence ☐ ☐ ☐ ☐ ☐

Computer Systems Knowledge

How do you rate yourself?

1	2	3	4	5

Keyboard skills ☐ ☐ ☐ ☐ ☐
Prescriptions ☐ ☐ ☐ ☐ ☐
Appointment system ☐ ☐ ☐ ☐ ☐
Registration of patients ☐ ☐ ☐ ☐ ☐
Keeps accurate computer records ☐ ☐ ☐ ☐ ☐

Personal Development - Things I need help on

Date / Page	Note of what you need help on (Tick as 'Done' when you've got the help)	Done
		☐
		☐
		☐
		☐
		☐
		☐
		☐
		☐
Speak to your manager or supervisor to get help on the topic		

4- Regulations and Safe Care

Who checks our quality?
Care involves many care and NHS bodies such as the Care Quality Commission (CQC), Social Services, Local Authorities, and Clinical Commissioning Groups.

Each of these want to ensure that people in our care are safe. They work closely with each other and may carry out their own inspections to make sure we are safe and provide good care.

What is an inspection?
An inspection can be a simple interview of the management or an in-depth review of systems and interviewing staff members. Inspections are designed to ensure that:-

1. A good standard of care was delivered in the past
2. A good standard of care will be delivered in the future
3. Management is well organised and competent
4. Staff are competent, skilled and knowledgeable
5. Stakeholders and clients know how we deliver care

What is CQC about?
CQC stands for Care Quality Commission. If you provide care, you need a licence to trade and this is the government body that issues these licences. Their inspections are in-depth to include all management and staff. Failing an inspection can result in cancelling the licence to trade and sometimes in prosecution.

Who does this apply to?
Every person working in care must meet quality standards and regulations. The law requires that anyone who fails to meet these standards should not be employed in care.

4.2- CQC – 5 Key Domains

Get to know what the CQC expect from us
Tick each one as you read them. Ask for help if you're not sure

Safe	By safe, we mean people are protected from abuse and avoidable harm. Abuse can be physical, sexual, mental or psychological, financial, neglect, institutional or discriminatory abuse	☐
Caring	By caring, we mean that the service involves and treats people with compassion, kindness, dignity and respect	☐
Responsive	By responsive, we mean that services meet people's needs.	☐
Effective	By effective, we mean that people's care, treatment and support achieves good outcomes, promotes a good quality of life and is based on the best available evidence.	☐
Well-Led	By well-led, we mean that the leadership, management and governance of the organisation assures the delivery of high-quality and person-centred care, supports learning and innovation and promotes an open and fair culture.	☐

Rate your confidence on this topic out of 5

1	2	3	4	5
☐	☐	☐	☐	☐

4.3 - Terminology you should know

Get to know these terms
Tick each one as you read them. Ask for help if you're not sure

CQC	The Care Quality Commission (CQC) is a government regulator for Healthcare and Adult Care. They monitor, inspect and regulate services to make sure they meet fundamental standards of quality and safety	☐
Carer	People who provide unpaid care by looking after their family, partners or friends who are in need of help because they are ill, frail, or have a disability	☐
Competent persons	People who have the required level of knowledge and skills for a particular task	☐
Compliance	Following the right process, and meeting rules and requirements	☐
Consent	A person's agreement to, or permission for any form of examination, care, treatment, or support	☐
Candour	This means being open and honest. When things go wrong, we are required to be honest and tell Service Users what happened and how we are fixing it	☐
Dignity	Treating people as being worthy of honour and respect, and listening to their views and beliefs	☐
Diversity	Understanding that each individual is unique and recognising our individual differences	☐

Effective	That the care, treatment and support we provide actually achieves good outcomes and a good quality of life	☐
Fit and Proper	That a person is of good character, honest, reliable, trustworthy and respectful. That they have the right qualifications, competence, skills and experience for the job	☐
Harm	Physical or psychological damage or injury	☐
Healthcare professional	Individuals regulated and/or licensed to provide some type of health or social care	☐
Human rights	The basic rights and freedoms contained in the European Convention on Human Rights	☐
Involvement	Involving people in the planning and delivery of their own care, treatment and support	☐
Mental health	A person's ability to manage and cope with the stresses and challenges of life	☐
Needs	All needs, including emotional, social, cultural, religious and spiritual needs	☐
Neglect	The failure to meet a person's basic physical and/or psychological needs	☐
Nominated individual	The person who is employed as a director or manager	☐

Nutritional and hydration needs	A person's need to receive suitable and nutritious food and hydration that is adequate to sustain life and good health	☐
Patient Safety Alerts	Alerts issued by the Central Alerting System on important public health messages and other safety critical information and guidance	☐
Personalised	Care or treatment provided to meet their particular needs and preferences	☐
Person-centred	Putting the person who uses services at the centre of their care	☐
Preferences	A person's preferences on how care and treatment are provided or which provider they choose to provide it	☐
Provider	An individual person, partnership or organisation registered with CQC	☐
Relevant person	the person using the service or a person acting on their behalf	☐
Respect	Treating people with care, compassion, with politeness, and equally with others	☐
Responsive	That services are organised so that they meet people's needs	☐
Risk	The likelihood of something going wrong	☐
Risk assessment	Identifying risks in any activity and assessing what could happen if things went wrong	☐
Safe	That people are protected from abuse and avoidable harm	☐

Safeguarding	To protect people from harm, abuse and neglect and ensuring good health, wellbeing, treatment and care	☐
Service user	The person who receives our services	☐
Social care	Personal care and other assistance provided for people who need this because of age, illness, disability, pregnancy, childbirth, or dependence on alcohol or drugs	☐
Staff	Everyone we employ in providing care and treatment	☐
Supervision	Guiding, supporting and helping other employees in their duties	☐
Timely	Acting as quickly as we can in providing care	☐
Treatment	Medical treatment, ongoing assessment, nursing and other care of a person	☐
Welfare	A person's condition, their physical, social and financial situation and their emotional and spiritual state	☐
Well-led	The leadership, management and governance of the organisation	☐

Do an overall rating of the topic once you have read 'Terminology you should know'

1	2	3	4	5

Rate your confidence on this topic out of 5   ☐ ☐ ☐ ☐ ☐

Regulations and Safe Care - Things I need help on

Date / Page	Note of what you need help on (Tick as 'Done' when you've got the help)	Done
		☐
		☐
		☐
		☐
		☐
		☐
		☐
		☐
Speak to your manager or supervisor to get help on the topic		

5- Knowledge & Training

Induction
This is an easy to follow refresher of your core knowledge and mandatory training. It is in a summary format as you will already have received a detailed induction and training to do your job right at the beginning.

Asking for help
1. If you need help on any topic, ask your manager or supervisor to explain
2. If you have forgotten old training, it is better to ask for fresh training
3. If something looks confusing, it is better to ask at the time and get it done right away

5.2- Being Professional

Skills and competency
Your skills and ability to work well make you a valued member of your team.
- Keep up to date with training and skills
- Try to improve your work
- People like working with skilled colleagues
- The better you are at your job, the more valued you become

Personal Conduct
Always maintain a high standard of conduct and work performance by:
- Observing rules, regulations and policies
- Treating colleagues with courtesy and respect
- Treating Service Users and visitors in a professional manner
- Working safely

Remember that the way you act with others reflects on our image as a team.

Accepting Gifts
People often like to thank us by giving gifts. This puts you in a difficult situation as others may see this as a bribe or people might then expect you to do favours in return.

To avoid this, whenever gifts are offered by anyone at all, the safest option is to refuse to take these in a polite way. If in doubt, ask your Manager for help. If anyone accepts bribes, they could be prosecuted under The Bribery Act.

1	2	3	4	5
☐	☐	☐	☐	☐

Rate your confidence on this topic out of 5

5.3- Recognising Risk

What is a Risk Assessment
You must be able to do risk assessments for situations you come across in your everyday work environment.
Most people think of risk assessments as a complex process that can only be done by experts, which is not correct, that is only true for very complex situations.

Every time you cross the road, you are actually doing a risk assessment of when it is safe to cross. If you are able to do this when your own life is at risk, then you must be able to do this with normal safety issues like fire prevention and delivering safe services.

Hazard Reviews
Hazard reviews are just another way of saying "look out for risks". It is a formal process of examining a situation to see if there are potential risks such as tripping over loose carpets, or flammable materials that might be a fire risk, or the way we are working is unsafe.

All staff should be aware of what risks are present in your environment and when you carry out tasks and whether there is a way to minimise the risk by better methods.

1	2	3	4	5
☐	☐	☐	☐	☐

Rate your confidence on this topic out of 5

5.4- Treating People with Care

Duty of Care
You are under a duty of care to the Service User. You must protect the Service User's interests at all times and thereby ensuring that your employer complies with its duty of care towards them and staff.

Dignity and Respect
Service Users must always be treated with dignity and respect. This is not only good practice, but it is also a legal requirement.
The way we act must show us to: -
- Be respectful to those in our care
- Prevent acts of discrimination and unfair treatment
- Be kind, supportive and understanding
- Be open and constructive in discussions
- Be fair and just in your dealings

Adequate Staff
Having adequate staff to operate efficiently is an essential requirement if we are to look after Service Users properly.
Each of us should be self-responsible for ensuring that we have an adequate team around us to deliver whatever care we are entrusted with at the time.
There are times when staff are stretched, and everyone has to work harder and longer. If this impacts on our ability to look after Service Users, it is important that this is reported to the manager for action.

Rate your confidence on this topic out of 5

1	2	3	4	5
☐	☐	☐	☐	☐

5.5- Choice and Preferences

Involvement in Care

We should involve Service Users in managing their own health, care and treatment.
This is to ensure that: -

- Treatment meets their actual needs
- These needs can be physical needs, emotional needs, social needs and cultural needs
- Service Users should be given all information required to help them make decisions
- We should meet their personal preferences wherever we can

We must ensure that reliable health information and advice is readily available to people under our care.

Mental Capacity Act

The Mental Capacity Act (MCA) is designed to protect and empower individuals who may lack the mental capacity to make their own decisions about their care and treatment. It is a law that applies to individuals aged 16 and over

Examples of people who may lack capacity include those with: -

- Dementia
- A severe learning disability
- A brain injury or stroke
- A mental health condition
- Unconsciousness caused by an anaesthetic or accident

The Act provides for exceptions when we have no choice but to override the need for consent, particularly when the Service User is unable or incapable of giving this consent.

1	2	3	4	5

Rate your confidence on this topic out of 5 ☐ ☐ ☐ ☐ ☐

5.6- Informed Consent

Informed Consent and decision making

The Service User should have sufficient information to enable them to make an informed decision about their treatment choices. Issues that must be covered during the decision-making process are: -

- Information about the pros and cons of all the treatment options, including non-treatment;
- Mental capacity of the Service User; decisions made under duress or undue influence;
- Whether the actions are the Service User's true wishes and in their best interest.

Informed Consent & Choice

Service Users have the right to:
- Choose their own GP practice, and to be accepted by that practice unless there are reasonable grounds to be refused
- Use a particular doctor within the practice, where possible
- Information and data on the quality of local healthcare providers, and on outcomes, compared to others.
- Information about the healthcare services available
- Easily accessible information in a form the Service User can understand.

Rate your confidence on this topic out of 5

1	2	3	4	5
☐	☐	☐	☐	☐

5.7- Sharing information

Sharing information with the right people can help to protect Service Users from harm and ensure that they get the help they need. It can also reduce the number of times they are asked the same questions by different professionals.

Service Users should:-

- Be able to express and have their views given due weight in all matters affecting them
- Be valued and respected as individuals
- Not be discriminated against

Our primary consideration is the best interests of the Service User. This applies to adults as well as children.

Rate your confidence on this topic out of 5

1	2	3	4	5
☐	☐	☐	☐	☐

5.8- Service User safety

Chaperone Policy
The presence of a third party does not negate the need for adequate explanation and courtesy and cannot provide full assurance that the procedure or examination is conducted appropriately.
To avoid any misunderstandings or distress and disruption caused by an allegation of inappropriate behaviour it is good practice to arrange for a chaperone when you perform an Intimate examination, even on a same-sex Service User.

Handover to other Professionals
Safeguarding and handover to other services go hand in hand. The person must be cared for at every stage from making an appointment, to care and treatment, and any follow up.
Each member of staff must ensure the utmost care and courtesy in their part of making the person's journey through care as safe and smooth as possible.

Identification of Carers
It is essential to establish whether Service Users have any carers, particularly when the Service User may be vulnerable.
Identify all carers, whether official or not, and make adequate note of this in their records. Carers can be family members or professional carers assigned by the local council or other bodies.

1	2	3	4	5
☐	☐	☐	☐	☐

Rate your confidence on this topic out of 5

5.9 - Incident Management

Incident Management

We must report all incidents that affect the health, safety and welfare of people who use services. This includes:-

- Injuries that may cause permanent or long-term damage
- Injuries or events that lead to psychological harm
- Any abuse or allegation of abuse
- Any incident which is reported to, or investigated by, the police
- Any event which affects our ability to operate safely
- Where we do not have sufficient staff to work safely
- Any major safety event that affects our premises for more than 24 hours

Rate your confidence on this topic out of 5

1	2	3	4	5
☐	☐	☐	☐	☐

5.10- Medicines Management

Medicines Management
Legal rules govern how medicines can be:
- Accessed
- Stored
- Produced
- Supplied
- Prescribed

Controlled Drugs
Clinical staff need a thorough knowledge of handling, storage, and destruction of controlled drugs.

Stricter legal controls apply to controlled medicines to prevent them:
- Being misused
- Being obtained illegally
- Causing harm

Everyone is responsible for following these principles, and those involved in dispensing and administering medicines need to ensure they have adequate training to carry out the treatment.

Rate your confidence on this topic out of 5

1	2	3	4	5
☐	☐	☐	☐	☐

5.11- Care Standards

Clinical Governance
If you are part of a clinical team, you should be familiar with the key components of clinical governance: -
1. Service User involvement
2. What Clinical Audits are
3. Evidence-based medical treatment
4. Managing risk in clinical treatments
5. Your Continuing Professional Development (CPD)

Staff Supervision
Supervision of staff is essential. Always ensure that there is appropriate supervision of care and clinical staff, particularly when newer or less experienced staff members are performing tasks and procedures that they are unfamiliar with.

Isolation of Service Users
There will be times when it is necessary to isolate some people in our care due to clinical conditions or simply to provide privacy. When providing a room where that Service User can wait, it must not be in any office where any sensitive data is available to view or where any consultations or anything medical or care related can be overheard or where they can wander undetected. This should also be away from staff areas.

1	2	3	4	5
☐	☐	☐	☐	☐

Rate your confidence on this topic out of 5

5.12- Prescriptions

Prescription security
Ensure that prescriptions are always secured under lock and key. Prescription forms should be treated as you would currency, a blank form is as good as bank note to some.

You should be aware of the procedures in your organisation to keep these secure at all times and the risks related to issues such as pre-signed forms, unattended forms, and access to unauthorised staff.

Prescribing Compliance
Clinical team members are required to regularly attend monthly prescribing meetings together with any quarterly reviews.
Prescribers are expected to attend the majority, if not all, of such meetings.
The objective is to review and reflect on our prescribing performance with regard to clinical appropriateness and cost effectiveness.
All discussions and outcomes must be minuted and documented along with an analysis of the source data.

Misuse of Prescriptions
All staff need to be vigilant of misuse of prescriptions.
Where there is a suspicion of misuse the person will be requested to attend a medication use review to discuss the use of items, and this may result in usage monitoring.
Any suspicion of misuse must be reported to your manager or GP if appropriate, and an "alert" should be placed in their records.

1	2	3	4	5
☐	☐	☐	☐	☐

Rate your confidence on this topic out of 5

5.13 - Safeguarding

Safeguarding Service Users
For an organisation, safeguarding means that you ensure you have:

- The right staff, properly trained
- Processes that hold everyone accountable for their actions
- A determined and effective leadership and management

We have a duty to protect all Service Users but need to exercise additional care in dealing with children and vulnerable adults

Who Needs Protection
Start with the rule of thumb that every Service User should be treated as needing to be protected.
Groups that need particular attention are Children and Vulnerable adults.
Always exercise particular care for:
- Anyone suffering from mental incapacity
- Anyone with age related or physical disability
- Anyone who has difficulty understanding their condition

1	2	3	4	5
☐	☐	☐	☐	☐

Rate your confidence on this topic out of 5

5.14- Abuse

What is abuse?
Abuse is 'The violation of an individual's human or civil rights by any other person or persons'.
Abuse may be a single act or repeated acts.
It may be physical, verbal or psychological, an act of neglect or an omission to act, or it may occur when a vulnerable person is persuaded to enter into a financial or sexual transaction to which he or she has not consented or cannot consent.
It may also occur through targeting or grooming of vulnerable people and may be carried out by individuals or groups of individuals.

Recognising abuse
Abuse can take on many forms e.g.
- Physical abuse
- Sexual abuse
- Emotional abuse
- Neglect
- Domestic abuse & violence
- Financial or material abuse
- Professional
- Bullying

1	2	3	4	5
☐	☐	☐	☐	☐

Rate your confidence on this topic out of 5

5.15- Vulnerable Persons

Vulnerable Children
It is unusual for a child not to be registered with a GP.
GPs remain the first point of contact for most health problems. This sometimes includes families who are not registered but seek medical attention.
A GP may be the first to recognise parental and or carer health problems, or behaviour in an individual which might pose a risk to children and young people.

Vulnerable Adults
A vulnerable adult is a person aged 18 years or over, who is in receipt of or may be in need of community care services by reason of:
- Mental or other disability
- Age or illness

This adult is or may be unable to take care of themselves, or unable to protect themselves against significant harm or exploitation.
It is important to remember that this covers the disabled and elderly.

Rate your confidence on this topic out of 5

1	2	3	4	5
☐	☐	☐	☐	☐

5.16 - When things go wrong

Blame-free culture
Nobody is perfect and even the best people make mistakes. When a mistake is made or an accident happens, we should not focus on who to blame but work out why it happened and if we can improve ourselves or the system so that this doesn't happen again.
This is called a "blame free culture".

Whistleblowing
Whistleblowing is the term used when someone passes on information concerning some wrongdoing. This is called "making a disclosure" or "blowing the whistle" and the wrongdoing will usually be something you have witnessed at work.
This can include: -
- Criminal offences and maybe financial fraud
- Failure to follow rules
- Endangering people's safety
- Damage to property or the environment
- Covering up wrongdoing

Rate your confidence on this topic out of 5

1	2	3	4	5
☐	☐	☐	☐	☐

5.17- Complaints

Handling Complaints
Complaint handling represents a valuable opportunity to gather information to make changes that deliver a better service and outcomes in the future.
When handling a complaint ensure that you try your best in:
- Helping to put things right
- Being customer focused
- Being open and accountable
- Acting fairly and proportionately
- Help in putting things right
- Learn from the complaints
- Seek continuous improvement

You must act properly, fairly and professionally at all times.
Always give the person complaining a copy of our Complaints Procedure.

Duty of Candour
Candour means being open and honest when things go wrong. Providers must promote a culture that encourages candour, openness, honesty and transparency at all levels.
When a notifiable safety incident has occurred, the relevant person must be informed as soon as reasonably possible after the incident has been identified. These are incidents that could result in, or appear to have resulted in, harm or prolonged psychological harm to a Service User.

Rate your confidence on this topic out of 5

1	2	3	4	5
☐	☐	☐	☐	☐

5.18- Emergencies & Serious incidents

Emergency incident procedure

Ensure you are familiar with our procedures on what to do in an emergency such as violent behaviour by a Service User.
Things you should be aware of:-

1. Taking precautionary measures if a Service User is known to be problematic.
2. Responding to incidents, panic buttons and alarms
3. Isolating the incident location and shielding other Service Users
4. Investigator's duties and how to handle issues

First Aid

It is important that all staff know the basics of first aid.
If you haven't received formal training, then ask your manager to arrange this for you
Ensure you know of which colleagues are fully trained and can be called upon in an emergency.

Handling Serious Untoward Incidents

Serious incidents are often triggered by events leading to serious outcomes for Service Users, staff and/or the organisation involved. If we see an incident occurring in another organisation delivering the care, then we should take action to inform them. We do this to ensure the incident is reported, investigated and learned from to prevent it happening again.

Rate your confidence on this topic out of 5

1	2	3	4	5
☐	☐	☐	☐	☐

5.19- Health & Safety

Health & Safety

Health and safety is about preventing injuries and illness through work. To achieve this every employee must follow safe practices. What you must do:-

- Follow the safety training you have been given
- Take care of your own and other people's health and safety.
- Tell someone (your supervisor or health and safety representative) if you think the work or inadequate precautions are putting anyone's health and safety at serious risk.

Dangerous Substances

COSHH (Control of Substances Hazardous to Health)

The law requires us to prevent exposure of staff and others, to substances hazardous to health e.g. clinical waste, microbiological agents, dusts of any kind in substantial quantities and all chemicals categorised as hazardous to health in any form i.e. solid, liquid, gas or vapour.

How to prevent exposure to hazardous substances: -

- Be vigilant about potential health hazards;
- Prevent harm by using risk assessments;
- Follow procedures that reduce harm to health;

Rate your confidence on this topic out of 5

1	2	3	4	5
☐	☐	☐	☐	☐

5.20- Safe Premises & Equipment

Premises

It is everyone's duty to ensure that premises are safe for Service Users and also our staff.

Spotting hazards like loose carpets, trips and slip hazards; sharp corners, and access to medicines are all common sense issues we can all look out for. In most cases, the person closest to the service is better placed to spot things out of place.

Be vigilant during your day to day work, correcting things where possible and reporting immediately anything that may cause harm to anyone using the premises.

Equipment

- All our equipment must be safe to use and safe for the person being treated.
- We use the term equipment to describe everything from electronics, lifting and clinical equipment and also furniture and furnishings.
- The person using equipment is most likely to spot malfunctioning or out of order equipment or loose wires and cables.
- Be vigilant; and always fix and report any equipment issues that might affect safety.

Rate your confidence on this topic out of 5

5.21 - Fire Safety

Fire and Environment

Every employee must co-operate to ensure the workplace is safe from fire and its effects and must not do anything that will place themselves or other people at risk.

In the event of a fire you should know:

- What to do on discovering a fire
- How to raise the alarm
- The procedures for alerting other staff, Service Users and visitors including directing them to exits
- The arrangements for calling the fire and rescue service
- The use of or the location of the fire-fighting equipment, escape routes and the assembly point
- How to open all emergency exit doors

Fire and smoke spread rapidly, often leaving only a few minutes to escape. Your thorough knowledge of a quick escape will be vital for you and persons in your care.

Rate your confidence on this topic out of 5

1	2	3	4	5
☐	☐	☐	☐	☐

5.22- Clinical Safety

Needlestick injuries
Always follow safety procedures to prevent needlestick injuries.
Immediate Action in case of injury:
- Make the wound bleed, if possible.
- Clean well with plenty of soap and running water.
- Apply occlusive dressing.
- Identify the source of the sharp and dispose of it properly.

Refer to a doctor first and liaise with the Consultant in communicable Disease Control and file an Accident Report.

Sharps use
It is a legal requirement that we minimise the use of sharps and to have protection measures in place.

All staff handling sharps must undergo training which covers the risk of injury and best practice as well as encouraging those healthcare workers at risk to be up to date with their vaccinations in the case of injury.

Do not handle sharps until you have received appropriate training.

Clinical Waste
Clinical waste is the term used to describe waste produced from healthcare and similar activities that may pose a risk of infection, for example, swabs, bandages, dressings etc. or may prove hazardous, for example medicines.

Clinical waste and healthcare waste may be hazardous or non-hazardous and needs to be separated from other types of waste and be treated/disposed of appropriately by specialist services.

1	2	3	4	5
☐	☐	☐	☐	☐

Rate your confidence on this topic out of 5

5.23- Your Personal Welfare

Workplace Stress

While some workplace stress is normal, too much stress can interfere with your productivity and affect your physical and emotional health. Here are some good coping strategies:

- Make your working conditions comfortable to work in
- Try to develop good relationships with your colleagues
- Get organised and plan ahead
- Learn to say no if you can't take on extra work or responsibility
- Take a walk or get some fresh air during the day
- Eat a balanced diet and try not to drink too much alcohol
- Work regular hours and take the breaks and holidays you're entitled to
- Maintain a healthy work-life balance

If you find that you are not coping talk to your manager

Bullying and Harassment

Bullying and harassment of any kind cannot be tolerated in the workplace.

Bullying may be characterised as offensive, intimidating, malicious or insulting behaviour, an abuse or misuse of power in ways that undermine, humiliate, or injure the recipient.

Harassment is any form of unwanted and unwelcome behaviour which may range from mildly unpleasant remarks to physical violence.

If you think you are being bullied, or see such behaviour, it is best to talk about it with your line manager or a senior person who will ensure appropriate steps are taken.

1	2	3	4	5
☐	☐	☐	☐	☐

Rate your confidence on this topic out of 5

5.24- Your Personal Safety

Lone Worker

When working alone or on home visits, keep colleagues informed. Each of us should watch out for anyone in that position. Basic rules to follow when working alone on the premises: -

1. Secure the building to prevent unauthorised entry.
2. Check phones are working and always carry a mobile phone.
3. Carry a list of emergency numbers, e.g. colleagues and police
4. Make sure at least one person is aware of your movements.
5. Check in regularly to keep them informed at all times.

When on home visits, ensure that the environment you are going into is safe to go in on your own e.g. locality, Service User's past history, known aggressors.
Always check if an alert has been placed on the clinical system.

Violence and Aggression

We do not tolerate any instances of work-related violence under any circumstances.
This includes incidents of abuse, threats or assault whether this is by other employees or a member of the public during the course of employment.
All employees have the right to be treated with consideration, dignity and respect.
You should report all incidents of violence and abuse immediately.
This policy applies to all staff working on our premises.

1	2	3	4	5
☐	☐	☐	☐	☐

Rate your confidence on this topic out of 5

5.25- Cleanliness

Cleanliness Vs Infection Control
Both of these are inter-related, and cleanliness will affect infection control.
The way we can understand the difference is: -
- Cleanliness is about stopping germs from growing
- Infection control is about stopping germs from spreading

Basic cleanliness
Cleanliness and hygiene are only part of the overall infection control regime. The basic principles do not require specialist training and much of this can be achieved by a common sense approach.
Important principles:
- Daily safety checks are the cornerstone of cleanliness and hygiene
- Every member of staff is responsible for observing cleanliness and hygiene in the workplace
- The organisation should encourage daily observation and monitoring by each member of staff, at least for their own area
- A rotation of the duty of daily safety checks will allow staff to experience leadership and prevention measures.

Rate your confidence on this topic out of 5

1	2	3	4	5
☐	☐	☐	☐	☐

5.26- Clean Premises and Equipment

Premises

Cleanliness and hygiene across all areas is the responsibility of all members of staff.

Although we may employ professional cleaners, the duty of care to our Service Users still remains our responsibility.

Always remember that infection control affects staff as much as the Service Users and that if things go wrong or we spot any potential issues, we must correct them immediately and report them to the manager.

Equipment

We take every care to ensure our equipment is safe, clean and infection-free to protect our Service Users during use.

Keeping non-clinical equipment clean and infection-free is just as vital as the rules for clinical equipment as infections can spread easily from one to the other.

All items of equipment are our tools of the trade, and being in daily use, require constant monitoring for cleanliness.

Equipment must be cleaned after every use, and any weaknesses in our process reported immediately.

Rate your confidence on this topic out of 5

1	2	3	4	5
☐	☐	☐	☐	☐

5.27 - Hand hygiene

Hand Hygiene

Good hand hygiene is the most important practice in reducing transmission of infectious agents

Hand hygiene includes routine hand washing, use of alcohol rubs/gels, hand care and surgical hand 'scrub'.

To ensure compliance with hand hygiene we must:

- Keep nails short, clean and polish free
- Avoid wearing wrist watches and jewellery e.g. rings etc.
- Not wear artificial nails or nail extensions
- Cover any cuts and abrasions with a waterproof dressing
- Comply with local dress code or uniform policy
- Report any skin conditions affecting hands

Rate your confidence on this topic out of 5

1	2	3	4	5
☐	☐	☐	☐	☐

5.28- Infection control

Infection Control

Clinical staff have a special responsibility for monitoring overall infection control.

In addition to managing clinical procedures, they must oversee how non-clinical staff follow standards

Clinicians carry the ultimate responsibility for all processes during clinical care and treatment

The issues they must understand, and control are all processes related to:-

- Sterilisation
- Cross contamination
- Spread of infection
- Handling of medicine
- Handling of samples
- Movement of Service Users during treatment.

Clinical

Every aspect of clinical care must be subject to the highest standards of cleanliness and infection control.

Staff must ensure they are fully versed with procedures on use of equipment, rules on disposable and reusable items, and the strict hygiene regime in consultations.

Always follow the special procedures in relation to equipment used in clinical care and report any issues immediately.

Rate your confidence on this topic out of 5

1	2	3	4	5
☐	☐	☐	☐	☐

5.29- Confidentiality & Caldicott

Duty of confidentiality

All employees are bound by a legal duty of confidentiality to protect personal information they come into
contact with during the course of their work.
This is not just a requirement of their contractual responsibilities but also a requirement within the common law duty of confidentiality and the Data Protection Act 1998. It is also a requirement within the NHS Care Record Guarantee if you work in the NHS.
Person-identifiable information is anything that contains the means to identify a person, e.g. name, address, postcode, date of birth or NHS number.

Confidentiality

- Safeguard the confidentiality of all person-identifiable or confidential information that you handle
- Clear your desk at the end of each day, keeping all portable records containing person-identifiable or confidential information in recognised filing and storage places
- Switch off computers and/or password protect them
- Secure transfers of person-identifiable or confidential information
- Challenge and verify where necessary the identity of any person who is making a request for confidential information
- Ensure that you cannot be overheard when discussing confidential matters
- Report any actual or suspected breaches of confidentiality

Rate your confidence on this topic out of 5

1	2	3	4	5
☐	☐	☐	☐	☐

5.30 - Confidentiality – Dos and Don'ts

When not to disclose
- When you don't have consent from the Service User to disclose their information
- When you are unsure about who you are disclosing the information to
- When you are asked to send data by email or internet to a non-NHS organisation.

Discussing Service Users
Ensure that you are in a secure environment when discussing any Service User related issues.
A common failing is discussion of Service User conditions in the reception area, within hearing distance of other people or in consulting rooms where people in adjoining rooms can overhear.

Confidentiality issues
We are bound by strict confidentiality codes to protect personal information and this is also a term of your contract of employment. You should never look up any information relating to your own family, friends or acquaintances unless you are directly involved in their care.
A breach of confidentiality constitutes gross misconduct and may result in dismissal.

1	2	3	4	5
☐	☐	☐	☐	☐

Rate your confidence on this topic out of 5

5.31- Records

Freedom of Information Act

The Freedom of Information Act 2000 gives any person legal rights of access to information which is held by a public authority.
Access to personal information is governed by the Data Protection Act 1998 and the request made under these provisions is known as a Subject Access request.
The person dealing with any requests for information must be qualified on how to deal with these regulations.

It is important to bear in mind that anything you record on the care records will be available to the Service User so exercise care in only recording factual and relevant information.

Incorrect information

Incorrect information will result in wrong treatment.
Any information must be accurate and delivered in a timely manner.
Information must be:
- Complete
- Accurate
- Relevant
- Accessible
- Timely

Rate your confidence on this topic out of 5

1	2	3	4	5
☐	☐	☐	☐	☐

5.32- Data Protection

Keeping data secure

- Don't share passwords or leave them lying around for others to see.
- Don't share information without the consent of the person to which the information relates, unless there are statutory grounds to do so.
- Don't use person-identifiable information unless absolutely necessary, anonymise the information where possible
- Don't collect, hold or process more information than you need, and do not keep it for longer than necessary.

Data Protection

All employees must:

- Observe all forms of guidance, codes of practice and procedures about the collection and use of personal information.
- Process appropriate information, and only for the purposes for which it is to be used
- Ensure the information is correctly entered in the system
- Ensure the information is destroyed appropriately when it is no longer required
- Understand that breaches of this Policy may result in disciplinary action, including dismissal

1	2	3	4	5
☐	☐	☐	☐	☐

Rate your confidence on this topic out of 5

5.33- Equality and Diversity

Who must Comply
Equality and Diversity rules apply to everyone you deal with as part of your job, not just workplace colleagues or Service Users.

Basic Rule
Do not disadvantage anyone based on their age, race, sex, gender reassignment status, disability, religion or belief, sexual orientation, marriage and civil partnership status, or pregnancy and maternity. It is your duty to protect people who are at risk of discrimination by association or perception.

Acting Unlawfully
Laws under the Equality Act set out that every Service User should be treated as an individual and with respect and dignity.
The laws mean that all organisations are required to make sure that services are fair and meet the needs of everyone, whatever their background or circumstances.

Consequences
Non-compliance might mean court or tribunal proceedings against us and will also affect our reputation.

This may also result in Disciplinary Action against staff members who have failed to follow rules.

Rate your confidence on this topic out of 5

1	2	3	4	5
☐	☐	☐	☐	☐

5.34- Discrimination

Age Discrimination

Age discrimination is about treating a person or employee less favourably because of their age.

It is unlawful to discriminate in any aspect of employment, including hiring, firing, pay, job assignments, promotions, layoff, training, benefits, and any other term or condition of employment.

Equal Opportunities

We should all ensure that no person or employee receives less favourable treatment on the grounds of sex, disability, religious belief, marital status, colour, race or ethnic origins, or is disadvantaged by conditions or requirements which cannot be shown to be justifiable.

All members of the organisation will be treated fairly and will not be discriminated against on any of the above grounds.

Decisions on recruitment and selection, training or any other benefit will be made objectively and based on aptitude and ability.

Rate your confidence on this topic out of 5

1	2	3	4	5
☐	☐	☐	☐	☐

Knowledge & Training - Things I need help on

Date / Page	Note of what you need help on (Tick as 'Done' when you've got the help)	Done
		☐
		☐
		☐
		☐
		☐
		☐
		☐
		☐
Speak to your manager or supervisor to get help on the topic		

6- Policies

Staff Centric Policies
These policies are simplified and in plain English to make them easy to read and easy to understand.

How to use this
1. There is an "abstract" at the top of each page, which is just a quick summary of what the policy says.
2. Reading the policy should take you about 1 minute in most cases.
3. If you don't understand something, use a pen to circle it or underline it. When you have time, ask your line manager to explain this.

Rate your achievement
1. Once you have read the policy, answer the questions on the next page under "Rate your achievement".
2. The rating is on a simple scale of 1 to 5, where 1 is lowest confidence and 5 is the highest confidence you have on this topic.
3. Don't forget that if something was not easy to understand at first, you can give it a low rating to start with. You can always come back and re-mark it as high after it has been explained to you.

6.2- Service Users

ABSTRACT
1. Treat Service Users equally without discrimination
2. Registering new Service Users is not simple
3. New users must always be dealt with by a suitably trained person

POLICY
Equality & Diversity:
Adapted from NHS Constitution handbook [Page 30]
Service Users have the right not to be unlawfully discriminated against in the provision of services on grounds of gender, race, disability, age, sexual orientation, religion, belief, gender reassignment, pregnancy and maternity or marital or civil partnership.

Registering New Service Users
Registering new Service Users is a complex process, and to be referred to someone who has been trained and authorised to do so They must be familiar with both the organisations latest policy on who we can and cannot take on, and our procedures on what checks must be carried out during this process.

The Service User may need to go through an interview process or examination and sometimes their immediate family or carers or social workers may need to be consulted.

Rate your achievement

Your level of confidence

How do you rate yourself?

1	2	3	4	5

I understand this policy ☐ ☐ ☐ ☐ ☐
I understand our procedures ☐ ☐ ☐ ☐ ☐
I am happy with my training on this ☐ ☐ ☐ ☐ ☐

Your confidence on what to do

Someone wants to register with us ☐ ☐ ☐ ☐ ☐
Who to ask if you are unsure ☐ ☐ ☐ ☐ ☐

When would you like your next training on this topic?

As soon as possible ☐
In 1 month ☐
In 3 months ☐
In 6 months ☐
In 12 months ☐

Your notes

6.3 - Appropriate Care

ABSTRACT
1. We should deliver the right care or refer to someone who can
2. We must have suitable and sufficient staff
3. You must have the right skills to deliver the care

POLICY
- We want to provide the right care.
- We must have suitable and sufficient staff.
- Service Users have the right to receive care and treatment that is appropriate for them, meets their needs and reflects their preferences

If you are tasked with the assessing a person's care, you must have the required levels of skill and knowledge for this particular task.

If you are not sure, always refer this to someone who is able to take over or help you with this task.

You must understand the difference between "Need for Care" and the "User's Preference"

1. Priority 1 is Need for Care: We should always provide the right care the user needs.
2. Priority 2 is User's Preference: To listen to preferences and meet these where possible.

Our aim is to ensure that
- Their care and treatment is well planned.
- Care plans are reviewed regularly and whenever necessary.
- If we cannot meet their needs and preferences, we must explain this and explore alternatives
- The Service user must be able to make informed decisions about their care and treatment.

Adapted from NHS Constitution handbook: [Page 24 & 140]

Rate your achievement

Your level of confidence

How do you rate yourself?

	1	2	3	4	5
I understand this policy	☐	☐	☐	☐	☐
I understand our procedures	☐	☐	☐	☐	☐
I am happy with my training on this	☐	☐	☐	☐	☐

Your confidence on what to do

	1	2	3	4	5
You can't cope due to staff shortages	☐	☐	☐	☐	☐
A team member seems unqualified	☐	☐	☐	☐	☐
Someone is not getting the right care	☐	☐	☐	☐	☐

When would you like your next training on this topic?

- As soon as possible ☐
- In 1 month ☐
- In 3 months ☐
- In 6 months ☐
- In 12 months ☐

Your notes

6.4 - Access to Care

ABSTRACT
1. Timely access to care is vital
2. The right care at the right time is important
3. Be aware if other care providers are not doing their job

POLICY
Care must be delivered in a timely manner and at the right time
Service Users must have ready access to care when needed

Timeliness of access to care will be different depending on the service being provided.

- Medical Care: Timely appointments and referrals
- Personal Care: The right staff should be available at the right time
- Home Visits: Staff being there at the appointed time

The Chain: Caring for a person is like a chain made of different providers
The chain breaks: If anyone fails to provide timely access and the right care at the right time.
What to look out for: When someone in this chain is failing to provide access to care in a timely manner.
Equality & Diversity
Service Users cannot be denied the right to access services because of their age, disability, race, gender or gender reassignment, sexual orientation, pregnancy and maternity, religion or belief, or marital or civil partnership status – these are all 'unreasonable grounds' on which to refuse access.

Adapted from NHS Constitution handbook: [Page 140]

Rate your achievement

Your level of confidence

How do you rate yourself?

1	2	3	4	5

	1	2	3	4	5
I understand this policy	☐	☐	☐	☐	☐
I understand our procedures	☐	☐	☐	☐	☐
I am happy with my training on this	☐	☐	☐	☐	☐

Your confidence on what to do

	1	2	3	4	5
Our team has missed an appointment	☐	☐	☐	☐	☐
Someone else missed an appointment	☐	☐	☐	☐	☐
A missed appointment caused distress	☐	☐	☐	☐	☐
Our team has missed an appointment					

When would you like your next training on this topic?

- As soon as possible ☐
- In 1 month ☐
- In 3 months ☐
- In 6 months ☐
- In 12 months ☐

Your notes

6.5 - Collaborative Care

ABSTRACT
1. Involve and work with other service providers
2. Make sure transition between services is smooth
3. Ensure the Service User and family are at the centre of care

POLICY
We must involve other services in handovers, referrals and transfers.
We must work well with other services.
All partner organisations should coordinate their health and social care services.

Adapted from NHS Constitution handbook: [Page 37]

- Care should centre on the person as a whole, not just on their specific condition
- Put the Service User, their family and carers at the centre of decisions that affect them
- Transition should be as smooth as possible when someone is referred between services
- Help Service Users to manage their own care, as far as they want and are able

Rate your achievement

Your level of confidence

How do you rate yourself?

	1	2	3	4	5
I understand this policy	☐	☐	☐	☐	☐
I understand our procedures	☐	☐	☐	☐	☐
I am happy with my training on this	☐	☐	☐	☐	☐

Your confidence on what to do

	1	2	3	4	5
We are not doing handovers properly	☐	☐	☐	☐	☐
Our teamwork is not very good	☐	☐	☐	☐	☐
Family members feel left out of decisions	☐	☐	☐	☐	☐

When would you like your next training on this topic?

- As soon as possible ☐
- In 1 month ☐
- In 3 months ☐
- In 6 months ☐
- In 12 months ☐

Your notes

6.6- Workplace Safety

ABSTRACT
1. Service Users must be kept safe
2. Staff must be kept safe
3. Our premises, equipment and environment must be safe

POLICY
Service Users must be cared for in a clean, safe, secure and suitable environment
Our staff must have a healthy and safe workplace
The workplace must be free from verbal or physical violence from patients, the public or other staff
Staff must be allowed to take annual holidays and to take regular breaks from work.

Adapted from NHS Constitution Handbook [page 40 & page 110]

A safe workplace environment means all of the following:-
- The Premises are safe
- Equipment is safe to use
- Small appliances are safe to use
- Electrical and gas safety is checked on a regular basis
- People have a safe environment free from abuse and violence

What you should do
- Keep an eye out for potential safety issues
- Fix things where you can
- Report potential safety issues to management
- Report immediately if something looks serious
- Report accidents and incidents
- Report near misses – where something could have gone wrong

Rate your achievement

Your level of confidence

How do you rate yourself?

	1	2	3	4	5
I understand this policy	☐	☐	☐	☐	☐
I understand our procedures	☐	☐	☐	☐	☐
I am happy with my training on this	☐	☐	☐	☐	☐

Your confidence on what to do

	1	2	3	4	5
You're worried about equipment safety	☐	☐	☐	☐	☐
Persons being abusive to staff	☐	☐	☐	☐	☐
Someone nearly tripped over	☐	☐	☐	☐	☐

When would you like your next training on this topic?

- As soon as possible ☐
- In 1 month ☐
- In 3 months ☐
- In 6 months ☐
- In 12 months ☐

Your notes

6.7 - Infection Control

ABSTRACT
1. Infection Control affects both Service Users and our staff
2. Cleanliness is about how each of us manages hygiene
3. It is about how the entire team works to prevent infections

POLICY

Service Users must be cared for in a clean, safe, secure and suitable environment.
Care must be delivered in clean premises with clean equipment.
A problem with infection control will affect everyone from Service Users to staff and visitors.
Adapted from NHS Constitution Handbook [page 40]

The Health and Social Care Act 2008 requires us to:-
- Provide and maintain a clean and appropriate environment
- Use the right antimicrobials to reduce the risk of infection
- Remember that infection safety affects everyone we come into contact with
- Identify people who are at risk of developing an infection
- If there is an infection outbreak, we should alert all Service Users, visitors and any person involved with providing further care as soon as possible

Things you should know well:
- Hand Hygiene
- Using Personal Protective Equipment
- Spillage Management

If your job requires, you should know about:-
- Safe Handling and Disposal of Sharps
- Safe Handling and Disposal of Chemicals and Hazardous Substances
- Safe Handling and Disposal of Clinical Waste

Rate your achievement

Your level of confidence

How do you rate yourself?

1	2	3	4	5

	1	2	3	4	5
I understand this policy	☐	☐	☐	☐	☐
I understand our procedures	☐	☐	☐	☐	☐
I am happy with my training on this	☐	☐	☐	☐	☐

Your confidence on what to do

	1	2	3	4	5
You notice unclean surfaces	☐	☐	☐	☐	☐
Cleaners haven't been in	☐	☐	☐	☐	☐
Someone's vomited on the floor	☐	☐	☐	☐	☐

When would you like your next training on this topic?

- As soon as possible ☐
- In 1 month ☐
- In 3 months ☐
- In 6 months ☐
- In 12 months ☐

Your notes

6.8- Medicines and Controlled Drugs

ABSTRACT
1. All drugs must be stored securely
2. Only authorised persons should have access
3. Only qualified persons can administer drugs

POLICY
For ALL staff
Be aware of control over and dispensing of drugs, even if this is not your main responsibility.
Issues to be aware of:-
- Drugs are stored securely
- Access is restricted to authorised persons only
- Controlled Drugs have very high security level and access rights
- Fridge Temperatures have to be monitored

For clinical and care staff
- Be aware of the strict rules over Controlled Drugs
- Make sure we observe rules over expiry dates and proper labelling
- Drugs should be administered by authorised and qualified persons
- Keep up to date with Medical Alerts

It is everyone's responsibility to be vigilant and report it immediately if you notice a breach of these rules

Rate your achievement

Your level of confidence

How do you rate yourself?

	1	2	3	4	5
I understand this policy	☐	☐	☐	☐	☐
I understand our procedures	☐	☐	☐	☐	☐
I am happy with my training on this	☐	☐	☐	☐	☐

Your confidence on what to do

	1	2	3	4	5
Drugs cabinet looks unlocked	☐	☐	☐	☐	☐
Medicines are left lying around	☐	☐	☐	☐	☐
Visitors can access the drugs cabinet	☐	☐	☐	☐	☐

When would you like your next training on this topic?

- As soon as possible ☐
- In 1 month ☐
- In 3 months ☐
- In 6 months ☐
- In 12 months ☐

Your notes

6.9- Fire Safety

ABSTRACT
1. Watch out for potential dangers or hazards
2. Report problems and fix if you can
3. Know how to respond to a fire

POLICY
Your life may depend on your knowledge of fire safety and evacuation procedures.
It is similar to insurance, you have to be prepared in advance just in case you need it.

Be vigilant every day for potential hazards such as:-
- Locked fire doors
- Entrances blocked by goods and rubbish
- Blocked exit routes
- Unsafe electrical equipment
- Flammable substances

If you spot a problem
- Report it to the manager
- Fix it if you can, especially minor things like blocked entrances

Responding to an actual fire
- Prepare for this now so you are ready if it happens
- You should know how to sound the alarm
- Know your means of escape, you might only have minutes
- Know the evacuation procedure and gathering points
- How will you help visitors who may not know all this
- We all need to be observant about their surroundings in daily life
- Watch out for others being careless, e.g. visitors and workers who don't know our rules

Rate your achievement

Your level of confidence

How do you rate yourself?

	1	2	3	4	5

I understand this policy ☐ ☐ ☐ ☐ ☐
I understand our procedures ☐ ☐ ☐ ☐ ☐
I am happy with my training on this ☐ ☐ ☐ ☐ ☐

Your confidence on what to do

You see boxes blocking the fire exit ☐ ☐ ☐ ☐ ☐
You have to find the evacuation plan ☐ ☐ ☐ ☐ ☐
There's a lock on the fire exit ☐ ☐ ☐ ☐ ☐

When would you like your next training on this topic?

As soon as possible ☐
In 1 month ☐
In 3 months ☐
In 6 months ☐
In 12 months ☐

Your notes

6.10- Recruitment Policy

ABSTRACT
1. Ensure your details are always up to date
2. Maintain your skills and personal development
3. Ensure you have relevant and sufficient skills for the job

POLICY
The Health and Social Care Act requires that we only employ Fit and Proper persons, and legally require us to have these for you.
Before you join:
- Proof of identity including a recent photograph
- Membership record of any professional body
- Documentary evidence of qualification for the job
- A full employment history and explanation of employment gaps
- Evidence of good conduct in previous employment
- Evidence of good conduct in relevant service
- Health information and declaration of fitness to carry out tasks for the job
- If you previously worked with children or vulnerable adults, provide reasons why you left
- For any previous convictions: A criminal record certificate

If any of the above is missing or has changed, you should tell us.
After you join:
- Make sure your personal records are up to date
- Make sure your skills fit the job you have been given
- Keep your skills up to date and ask if you need help or training
- You should not be discriminated against, and you should not discriminate against others

Tick the items below to declare your compliance:-
- ☐ You are fit and healthy to do your job
- ☐ Nothing has happened that affects your DBS record

Rate your achievement

Your level of confidence

How do you rate yourself?

	1	2	3	4	5
I understand this policy	☐	☐	☐	☐	☐
I understand our procedures	☐	☐	☐	☐	☐
I am happy with my training on this	☐	☐	☐	☐	☐

Your confidence on what to do

	1	2	3	4	5
Something affects your DBS	☐	☐	☐	☐	☐
Your address has changed	☐	☐	☐	☐	☐
You're given a task but not trained for it	☐	☐	☐	☐	☐

When would you like your next training on this topic?

- As soon as possible ☐
- In 1 month ☐
- In 3 months ☐
- In 6 months ☐
- In 12 months ☐

Your notes

6.11 - Equal Opportunities

ABSTRACT
1. You will not be discriminated against in your employment
2. You must treat other members of the team in the same way
3. You must behave the same with anyone else we work with or collaborate with

POLICY
Adapted from NHS Constitution handbook [Page 30]
Everyone has the right not to be unlawfully discriminated against on grounds of gender, race, disability, age, sexual orientation, religion, belief, gender reassignment, pregnancy and maternity or marital or civil partnership status.

Equal opportunities apply to everyone working in our organisation. Sometimes you will have a boss, and at other times you will be the boss for junior staff.

Responsibilities of the employer
You should be treated fairly and given an equal opportunity in your job and any opportunities available in the organisation.

Responsibilities of team members
The principles of equal opportunity extend to your interaction with:-
- Other team members and colleagues
- Subordinates and staff you are supervising
- External persons you work with or collaborate with

Rate your achievement

Your level of confidence

How do you rate yourself?

1	2	3	4	5

	1	2	3	4	5
I understand this policy	☐	☐	☐	☐	☐
I understand our procedures	☐	☐	☐	☐	☐
I am happy with my training on this	☐	☐	☐	☐	☐

Your confidence on what to do

	1	2	3	4	5
Someone's being discriminated against	☐	☐	☐	☐	☐
You feel discriminating against	☐	☐	☐	☐	☐

When would you like your next training on this topic?

- As soon as possible ☐
- In 1 month ☐
- In 3 months ☐
- In 6 months ☐
- In 12 months ☐

Your notes

6.12- Staff Sufficiency & Suitability

ABSTRACT
1. You should have the right skills for the job
2. Keep your skills and training up to date
3. Always ask for help if you need training, development, or support

POLICY
Service Users have the right to be treated with a professional standard of care, by appropriately qualified and experienced staff, in a properly approved or registered organisation that meets required levels of safety and quality.

Adapted from NHS Constitution Handbook [page 38]

Employer's responsibilities
- Have the right person for the right job
- Provide training and support to do the job
- Provide opportunities to develop skills
- Have sufficient staff to meet service requirements

Your responsibilities
- You are suitably qualified to do the job
- You have the skills to do the job, and you keep these up to date
- Ask for help if you feel you are having difficulties or feel out of your depth
- Complete your training when asked
- Keep a record of all your training and learning activities

If there is insufficient staff to carry out the tasks, you should bring this to the attention of your manager. All organisations suffer shortages from time to time, and the objective is to work together as a team to overcome problems.

Rate your achievement

Your level of confidence

How do you rate yourself?

	1	2	3	4	5
I understand this policy	☐	☐	☐	☐	☐
I understand our procedures	☐	☐	☐	☐	☐
I am happy with my training on this	☐	☐	☐	☐	☐

Your confidence on what to do

	1	2	3	4	5
We can't cope without additional staff	☐	☐	☐	☐	☐
Someone can't do their job properly	☐	☐	☐	☐	☐
You're not fully trained for your job	☐	☐	☐	☐	☐

When would you like your next training on this topic?

- As soon as possible ☐
- In 1 month ☐
- In 3 months ☐
- In 6 months ☐
- In 12 months ☐

Your notes

6.13- Professional Development

ABSTRACT
1. Maintaining your skills is necessary for you to continue to do a good job
2. Personal development makes you better at the job
3. Everyone appreciates working with a good performer

POLICY
Continuing Professional Development (CPD) is important for you because:
- It helps maintain your skills
- Improves your skills to make you a better performer
- Keeps you motivated
- Gives you job satisfaction
- Learning is key to progression in your career

Benefits of a well qualified team:-
- Improves our services
- We have better quality standards
- Everyone feels valued
- Better job satisfaction
- Sense of achievement

It is easier to work with colleagues who know what they are doing and are competent at their job. To be valued in the same way, the more you make personal improvements, the more other team members will appreciate working with you.

Rate your achievement

Your level of confidence

How do you rate yourself?

1	2	3	4	5

	1	2	3	4	5
I understand this policy	☐	☐	☐	☐	☐
I understand our procedures	☐	☐	☐	☐	☐
I am happy with my training on this	☐	☐	☐	☐	☐

Your confidence on what to do

	1	2	3	4	5
There's no time to do your training	☐	☐	☐	☐	☐
You need feedback on your performance	☐	☐	☐	☐	☐
You don't know how to improve	☐	☐	☐	☐	☐

When would you like your next training on this topic?

- As soon as possible ☐
- In 1 month ☐
- In 3 months ☐
- In 6 months ☐
- In 12 months ☐

Your notes

6.14- Bullying and Harassment

ABSTRACT
1. No one should bully or harass you
2. You should not bully or harass anyone else
3. You must report this if you or anyone else is subjected to this

POLICY
Everyone must be able to work in an environment free from bullying and harassment.
We should all be treated, and treat others, with dignity and respect.
Any bullying to you or someone else must be reported immediately
What is bullying
Offensive, intimidating, malicious or insulting behaviour.
Abuse or misuse of power or actions that undermine, humiliate, or injure a person or their feelings. Examples:-
- Physical or psychological threats;
- Overbearing and intimidating levels of supervision;
- Derogatory remarks about a person or their performance

What is harassment
This can be any form of unwanted and unwelcome behaviour which may range from mildly unpleasant remarks to physical violence.
Some examples of harassment:
- Unwanted physical conduct including touching, pinching, pushing and grabbing
- Unwelcome sexual advances or suggestive behaviour
- Offensive e-mails, text messages or social media content or the display of offensive materials
- Unwanted jokes, banter, mocking, mimicking or belittling a person

Rate your achievement

Your level of confidence

How do you rate yourself?

1	2	3	4	5

	1	2	3	4	5
I understand this policy	☐	☐	☐	☐	☐
I understand our procedures	☐	☐	☐	☐	☐
I am happy with my training on this	☐	☐	☐	☐	☐

Your confidence on what to do

	1	2	3	4	5
Someone is being bullied	☐	☐	☐	☐	☐
You are being bullied	☐	☐	☐	☐	☐
Someone makes insulting comments	☐	☐	☐	☐	☐

When would you like your next training on this topic?

- As soon as possible ☐
- In 1 month ☐
- In 3 months ☐
- In 6 months ☐
- In 12 months ☐

Your notes

6.15- Whistleblowing

ABSTRACT
1. You can report misconduct and concerns to the top, instead of your line manager
2. You should feel safe from "revenge" when reporting misconduct
3. You are protected by law from revenge and persecution

POLICY

'Whistleblowing' means the reporting by employees of suspected misconduct, illegal acts or failure to act within the organisation.

The ability to report misconduct incidents without fear of revenge helps the organisation learn from their failures and improve how they take care of their staff and quality of care.

Whistle-blowers are protected by law to prevent them being persecuted just because they care enough to want to improve things.

Examples of things you can report:
- A criminal offence, for example fraud
- Someone's health and safety is in danger
- Risk of, or actual damage to the environment
- A miscarriage of justice
- The organisation breaking the law, for example does not have the right insurance
- You believe someone is covering up wrongdoing

You should be able to report misconduct directly "to the top" if your line manager cannot adequately deal with the issue or where you feel that an independent person in the organisation needs to investigate the issue.

Rate your achievement

Your level of confidence

How do you rate yourself?

	1	2	3	4	5
I understand this policy	☐	☐	☐	☐	☐
I understand our procedures	☐	☐	☐	☐	☐
I am happy with my training on this	☐	☐	☐	☐	☐

Your confidence on what to do

	1	2	3	4	5
Someone's deliberately breaking rules	☐	☐	☐	☐	☐
People are taking risks in their work	☐	☐	☐	☐	☐
Someone did something illegal	☐	☐	☐	☐	☐

When would you like your next training on this topic?

- As soon as possible ☐
- In 1 month ☐
- In 3 months ☐
- In 6 months ☐
- In 12 months ☐

Your notes

6.16- Disciplinary and Grievance

ABSTRACT
1. Grievance is about resolving a work issue in a fair way
2. Disciplinary Action is where someone thinks you might have done something serious
3. The process must be fair and both parties have a chance to put their side of the story

POLICY

What is Grievance
- You have a complaint about your employment that you would like resolved
- You want a fair hearing and a just outcome
- You want someone independent to look at your case

A Grievance procedure is usually started by a person who has a problem they would like resolved, so they can go back to doing their job as before.

What is Disciplinary Action
- When someone thinks you have done something serious such as breach of rules
- Both sides are given a chance to put their side of the story
- It needs a proper investigation and looking into the facts
- Someone will look into this to see if the allegations are true
- The process should be fair
- Action is only taken if the allegations are true

How should these be dealt with (From the ACAS code of practice)
- Issues should be dealt with fairly and with transparency
- Deal with issues promptly and act consistently.
- A proper investigation to establish the facts
- Meetings to discuss the problem
- An opportunity for both sides to put their case
- Provide an opportunity to appeal any decision.

Rate your achievement

Your level of confidence

How do you rate yourself?

	1	2	3	4	5
I understand this policy	☐	☐	☐	☐	☐
I understand our procedures	☐	☐	☐	☐	☐
I am happy with my training on this	☐	☐	☐	☐	☐

Your confidence on what to do

	1	2	3	4	5
You're not happy how you are treated	☐	☐	☐	☐	☐
You are accused of serious misconduct	☐	☐	☐	☐	☐

When would you like your next training on this topic?

- As soon as possible ☐
- In 1 month ☐
- In 3 months ☐
- In 6 months ☐
- In 12 months ☐

Your notes

6.17- Care and Planning

ABSTRACT
1. Service Users should be involved in their care plan.
2. Planning should include all other parties involved in that care
3. Care should be personalised to the Service User's needs

POLICY

Service Users have the right to be involved in planning and making decisions about their health and care, including end of life care. This can include their family, various healthcare professionals and carers. Service Users should be given a chance to manage their own care and treatment where possible.

Service Users have the right to receive suitable and nutritious food and hydration to sustain good health and wellbeing.

Adapted from NHS Constitution Handbook [page 75 & 42]

- Care planning is the process of assessing, agreeing, collaborating and supporting an individual in their care.
- This should be done in plain language so that everyone understands.
- Service users and carers should be able to personalise care to their own needs.
- It is important to collaborate with all stakeholders and care providers.

Rate your achievement

Your level of confidence

How do you rate yourself?

	1	2	3	4	5
I understand this policy	☐	☐	☐	☐	☐
I understand our procedures	☐	☐	☐	☐	☐
I am happy with my training on this	☐	☐	☐	☐	☐

Your confidence on what to do

	1	2	3	4	5
There is no care plan for a Service User	☐	☐	☐	☐	☐
Service User says "I'm kept in the dark"	☐	☐	☐	☐	☐
	☐	☐	☐	☐	☐

When would you like your next training on this topic?

- As soon as possible ☐
- In 1 month ☐
- In 3 months ☐
- In 6 months ☐
- In 12 months ☐

Your notes

6.18- Duty of Candour & Openness

ABSTRACT
1. Be open with Service Users about things that went wrong
2. Explain what went wrong and if there was any harm
3. We must support them and resolve the issue

POLICY

Service Users have the right to an open and transparent relationship with us.

They must be told about any safety incident relating to their care which may have or could have caused harm.

They must be given the facts, an apology, and any reasonable support needed.

We should aim to be open with Service Users, their families, carers or representatives if anything goes wrong.

We should welcome feedback and address concerns promptly and in a spirit of co-operation.

Adapted from NHS Constitution Handbook [page 77 & page 147]

This is how we should meet our obligation:

- Tell Service User when things have gone wrong
- Be open and transparent in relation to care
- Explain to the Service User what's known at the time
- Clarify what further enquiries will be made
- Offer an apology if needed
- Provide the Service User with a written note of any discussions
- Keep a written record of all correspondence
- Provide all reasonable support such as an interpreter or emotional counselling

Duty of candour is a legal requirement for all care providers, and it is a criminal offence if we don't comply

Rate your achievement

Your level of confidence

How do you rate yourself?

	1	2	3	4	5
I understand this policy	☐	☐	☐	☐	☐
I understand our procedures	☐	☐	☐	☐	☐
I am happy with my training on this	☐	☐	☐	☐	☐

Your confidence on what to do

	1	2	3	4	5
Who handles complaints we receive	☐	☐	☐	☐	☐
Who keeps you informed about safety	☐	☐	☐	☐	☐
Who manages serious incidents	☐	☐	☐	☐	☐

When would you like your next training on this topic?

- As soon as possible ☐
- In 1 month ☐
- In 3 months ☐
- In 6 months ☐
- In 12 months ☐

Your notes

6.19- Intimate, Physical Care & Chaperone

ABSTRACT
1. Intimate care can be embarrassing and distressing
2. We must obtain consent before any intimate care is provided
3. Using a Chaperone provides reassurance and avoids allegations of misconduct

POLICY

Service Users have the right to accept or refuse treatment that is offered.

We must obtain valid consent before any physical examination or treatment.

We need to be sure they have the capacity to give consent or obtain this from a person legally able to act on their behalf.

Adapted from NHS Constitution Handbook [page 55]

Using a Chaperone avoids any misunderstanding or distress caused by an allegation of inappropriate behaviour.

Chaperones should be offered before any intimate examination or care provision; even on a same-sex Service User.

What you should know about Chaperoning:
- We need to get consent before any examination or intimate care provision
- A chaperone should be offered in intimate examinations
- Chaperones have to be properly trained
- Always keep a record of what was offered, what was agreed, and if all went well

Rate your achievement

Your level of confidence

How do you rate yourself?

	1	2	3	4	5
I understand this policy	☐	☐	☐	☐	☐
I understand our procedures	☐	☐	☐	☐	☐
I am happy with my training on this	☐	☐	☐	☐	☐

Your confidence on what to do

	1	2	3	4	5
How to offer chaperone service	☐	☐	☐	☐	☐
Who does the chaperoning for us	☐	☐	☐	☐	☐

When would you like your next training on this topic?

- As soon as possible ☐
- In 1 month ☐
- In 3 months ☐
- In 6 months ☐
- In 12 months ☐

Your notes

6.20 - Health, Nutrition & Wellbeing

ABSTRACT
1. Adequate nutrition for a Service User is a legal requirement
2. Be aware if it is our duty to ensure nutritional requirements
3. Be observant if someone else is supposed to provide this

POLICY
Nutrition and hydration:

If we provide the food and drink:
We should take care to ensure that the Service User is properly fed and looked after.
Looking after their diet needs means:-
- Providing the right food and drink
- Proving the right amounts for their needs

Every Service User will have different needs, and it is part of our duty to provide personalised care.

If someone else provides the food and drink:
- Be observant about the Service User's condition
- Each of us needs to look after the Service User's interests
- Look out for signs if someone else is not doing a good job
- Report any concerns or suspicions of neglect to your manager or clinical staff

Rate your achievement

Your level of confidence

How do you rate yourself?

	1	2	3	4	5
I understand this policy	☐	☐	☐	☐	☐
I understand our procedures	☐	☐	☐	☐	☐
I am happy with my training on this	☐	☐	☐	☐	☐

Your confidence on what to do

	1	2	3	4	5
Someone looks really under nourished	☐	☐	☐	☐	☐
User complains they get little food	☐	☐	☐	☐	☐

When would you like your next training on this topic?

- As soon as possible ☐
- In 1 month ☐
- In 3 months ☐
- In 6 months ☐
- In 12 months ☐

Your notes

6.21- Safeguarding

ABSTRACT
1. It is our duty to help safeguard vulnerable people
2. It is our duty to recognise and report suspicion of abuse
3. Always report any concerns and suspicions

POLICY
Service Users have the right to be protected from abuse and neglect, or care and treatment that is degrading.

Adapted from NHS Constitution Handbook [page 54]

Safeguarding
Safeguarding children, young people and adults at risk is a shared responsibility between us, other agencies and professionals involved in their care.
What you should know about safeguarding:
- Recognising who might be at risk
- This is covered in your training and continuing professional development
- Who is the Safeguarding Lead or Responsible Person in our organisation?

Abuse
This is the violation of a person's rights by another person
It can be a single act or repeated acts.
It can happen through targeting or grooming of vulnerable people and may be carried out by individuals or groups of people.
Types of abuse
- Physical, emotional, sexual or neglect
- Domestic abuse and violence
- Financial and material abuse
- Professional, institutional and bullying in a workplace

Rate your achievement

Your level of confidence

How do you rate yourself?

	1	2	3	4	5
I understand this policy	☐	☐	☐	☐	☐
I understand our procedures	☐	☐	☐	☐	☐
I am happy with my training on this	☐	☐	☐	☐	☐

Your confidence on what to do

	1	2	3	4	5
You think someone is being abused	☐	☐	☐	☐	☐
Who should you report abuse to	☐	☐	☐	☐	☐

When would you like your next training on this topic?

- As soon as possible ☐
- In 1 month ☐
- In 3 months ☐
- In 6 months ☐
- In 12 months ☐

Your notes

6.22 - Managing Mental Health & Disability

ABSTRACT
1. Take care if people have mental health and disability issues
2. Getting consent for care and treatment will be challenging
3. Sometimes we have to make decisions for them, even without consent

POLICY

We can only provide good care if both parties fully understand each other about the problems they have and what care we will provide. This can be difficult when they do not have the capacity to understand.

You should be able to recognise when they have limited capacity to make decisions and must exercise greater care.

This is important when we are dealing with:-
- Vulnerable adults or children
- Persons with special needs and learning difficulties
- Persons with disabilities
- Persons with conditions like dementia

The Mental Capacity Act protects vulnerable persons. It also says that sometimes we have no choice but to override the need for consent, for example:-
- They are 16 or over but still not capable of giving consent.
- They can't give consent because of an emergency situation
- When they are in our accommodation, we have to make decisions for them for proper nutrition or hydration
- Different rules apply for Service Users in custody or in prison

All clinical and care staff should be aware of issues regarding capability of consent and deprivation of liberty under Section 4 of the Mental Capacity Act 2005

Rate your achievement

Your level of confidence

How do you rate yourself?

	1	2	3	4	5
I understand this policy	☐	☐	☐	☐	☐
I understand our procedures	☐	☐	☐	☐	☐
I am happy with my training on this	☐	☐	☐	☐	☐

Your confidence on what to do

	1	2	3	4	5
Talk to persons with learning disabilities	☐	☐	☐	☐	☐
How to help persons with dementia	☐	☐	☐	☐	☐
You're asked what a vulnerable adult is?	☐	☐	☐	☐	☐

When would you like your next training on this topic?

- As soon as possible ☐
- In 1 month ☐
- In 3 months ☐
- In 6 months ☐
- In 12 months ☐

Your notes

6.23 - Prescriptions Management

ABSTRACT
1. Prescription security is vital
2. Used and unused forms must be kept under lock and key
3. Work as a team to be vigilant and prevent mishaps

POLICY
We should all work together to ensure best practice in prescription handling and security.
Treat prescription forms as you would currency, a blank form is as good as bank note to some.
Ensure that you know who the responsible person is for managing prescriptions.

How clinical staff have to manage prescriptions:
- Keep a record of the serial numbers of prescription forms
- Never pre-sign blank prescriptions
- Keep unused stock under lock and key
- Prescription should only be accessible to authorised staff
- Surgery stamps are like a signature and should be kept in a secure location
- Completed forms should be stored in locked drawer/cabinet

How Home/Care home visit staff have to manage prescriptions:
- Take precautions to prevent the loss or theft of forms
- Record the serial numbers of any prescription forms/pads they are carrying
- Keep forms out of sight when not in use
- Never leave prescription forms in vehicles overnight

If you see a breach of rules:
- Take control of any loose prescription forms
- Report it immediately to the manager or responsible person
- Hand the prescription to the right person

Rate your achievement

Your level of confidence

How do you rate yourself?

	1	2	3	4	5

	1	2	3	4	5
I understand this policy	☐	☐	☐	☐	☐
I understand our procedures	☐	☐	☐	☐	☐
I am happy with my training on this	☐	☐	☐	☐	☐

Your confidence on what to do

	1	2	3	4	5
You see blank prescriptions lying around	☐	☐	☐	☐	☐
Who to report to about prescriptions	☐	☐	☐	☐	☐

When would you like your next training on this topic?

- As soon as possible ☐
- In 1 month ☐
- In 3 months ☐
- In 6 months ☐
- In 12 months ☐

Your notes

6.24 - Informed Consent

ABSTRACT
1. Service Users must be given all information to make an informed decision of their care
2. Consent is a continuing consultation, and the Service User is allowed to change their mind
3. Responsible Persons must always be involved. This can mean family and other carers.

POLICY
Service Users have the right to be given information about the test and treatment options available to them, what they involve and their risks and benefits.
Valid consent to treatment is absolutely central to all care provision.

Adapted using NHS Constitution Handbook [page 57]

What is consent
Consent is a process not just a one-off decision. The steps in the process include discussions, the giving of verbal and written information and the explanation of risks and benefits and consequences of proposed treatment.

- Before treatment starts, we must obtain consent to the care and treatment from the Service User or their guardian/carer.
- They also need to know how to change decisions about things that have been agreed previously.
- Service users must be given full information about their condition and the treatment options available to them.

Sometimes it is necessary to provide treatment without consent if it is an emergency or where the Service User is unable to make the decision.

Rate your achievement

Your level of confidence

How do you rate yourself?

1	2	3	4	5

I understand this policy ☐ ☐ ☐ ☐ ☐
I understand our procedures ☐ ☐ ☐ ☐ ☐
I am happy with my training on this ☐ ☐ ☐ ☐ ☐

Your confidence on what to do

Who is responsible to do this ☐ ☐ ☐ ☐ ☐
Who to ask about this ☐ ☐ ☐ ☐ ☐

When would you like your next training on this topic?

As soon as possible ☐
In 1 month ☐
In 3 months ☐
In 6 months ☐
In 12 months ☐

Your notes

6.25 - Involvement in Care

ABSTRACT
1. We want to support self-management of care by the Service User
2. We want to enable people to make informed health decisions
3. We want to provide person-centred care

POLICY
Service Users have the right to be involved, directly or through representatives, in the planning of their care.

Service Users should be able to make informed choices, including information about the available options and the risks and benefits associated with each option.

Adapted from NHS Constitution Handbook [pages 78 & 80]

- We should help people to manage and make informed decisions about their own health and care.
- We must offer person-centred care tailored to the needs of the individual.
- All providers, healthcare professionals and other stakeholders should work collaboratively with people who use the services.

Rate your achievement

Your level of confidence

How do you rate yourself?

1	2	3	4	5

I understand this policy ☐ ☐ ☐ ☐ ☐
I understand our procedures ☐ ☐ ☐ ☐ ☐
I am happy with my training on this ☐ ☐ ☐ ☐ ☐

Your confidence on what to do

Who is responsible to do this ☐ ☐ ☐ ☐ ☐
Who to ask about this ☐ ☐ ☐ ☐ ☐

When would you like your next training on this topic?

As soon as possible ☐
In 1 month ☐
In 3 months ☐
In 6 months ☐
In 12 months ☐

Your notes

6.26- Provision of Lifestyle

ABSTRACT
1. A person's lifestyle affects their health
2. We should help them understand and persuade them to make the right choices
3. We should give them information to help them make the right choices

POLICY

A person's lifestyle has a direct effect on their health.
We cannot force people to change poor habits, but they may change them if they understand the problem.
We should help them by giving advice and information about how their lifestyles are affecting their health.

Clinical and care staff are responsible for guiding the Service User
All staff should know about leaflets available and who is qualified to give guidance.
Examples of information for Service Users:-
- How to improve their diet and reduce weight;
- How to reduce blood pressure;
- Reducing stress;
- Ways to quit smoking;
- The benefits of exercise;
- The benefits of reducing alcohol consumption;
- How to improve sexual health;
- How to check for symptoms of common cancers such as testicular and breast cancer;
- Local support programmes and how to refer people

Even if you are not directly involved in giving guidance, you should be able to explain what help we provide and the team members you can refer them to.
[Adapted from British Medical Association guidelines]

Rate your achievement

Your level of confidence

How do you rate yourself?

1	2	3	4	5

I understand this policy ☐ ☐ ☐ ☐ ☐
I understand our procedures ☐ ☐ ☐ ☐ ☐
I am happy with my training on this ☐ ☐ ☐ ☐ ☐

Your confidence on what to do

You're asked, "How do you do this?" ☐ ☐ ☐ ☐ ☐
Who is responsible for this ☐ ☐ ☐ ☐ ☐

When would you like your next training on this topic?

As soon as possible ☐
In 1 month ☐
In 3 months ☐
In 6 months ☐
In 12 months ☐

Your notes

6.27 - Dignity & Respect

ABSTRACT
1. Be respectful and fair to everyone
2. Prevent discrimination and bad conduct
3. Be supportive and open to discussion

POLICY
Adapted from NHS Constitution handbook [Page 30]
Service Users have the right not to be unlawfully discriminated against in the provision of services on grounds of gender, race, disability, age, sexual orientation, religion, belief, gender reassignment, pregnancy and maternity or marital or civil partnership status.

All Service Users, employees and visitors have the right to be treated with consideration, dignity and respect.

How we should work:
- Be respectful to everyone
- Prevent acts of discrimination and unfair treatment
- Be kind and supportive and understanding
- Be open and constructive in discussions
- Be fair and just in your dealings

Unacceptable Behaviour
Behaviour of a physical, verbal or non- verbal kind which is not acceptable:
- Something that is likely to offend
- Intimidating, hostile or humiliating actions
- Lack of respect
- Threats or threatening behaviour

Rate your achievement

Your level of confidence

How do you rate yourself?

	1	2	3	4	5
I understand this policy	☐	☐	☐	☐	☐
I understand our procedures	☐	☐	☐	☐	☐
I am happy with my training on this	☐	☐	☐	☐	☐

Your confidence on what to do

	1	2	3	4	5
Staff being rude to people	☐	☐	☐	☐	☐
Someone is being treated badly	☐	☐	☐	☐	☐

When would you like your next training on this topic?

- As soon as possible ☐
- In 1 month ☐
- In 3 months ☐
- In 6 months ☐
- In 12 months ☐

Your notes

6.28- Access to Records

ABSTRACT
1. Service Users have a right to access and correct their records
2. Be aware of the need to observe confidentiality, data protection, and security of records
3. Always refer to the person authorised to verify and release information

POLICY
Service Users have a right to access their own health records and to have any factual inaccuracies corrected.

Adapted using NHS Constitution Handbook [page 58]

Service Users have legal rights to access their personal data.
- Be aware of who is the Designated Person for GDPR and data protection if you need help
- Pass on all enquiries to the person authorised to release confidential information

What we need to do:-
- Ensure that records are correct, accurate and truthful
- Only enter relevant information without personal comments
- Do not hand out records unless you are authorised to do so
- Observe strict confidentiality at all times

Rate your achievement

Your level of confidence

How do you rate yourself?

1	2	3	4	5

	1	2	3	4	5
I understand this policy	☐	☐	☐	☐	☐
I understand our procedures	☐	☐	☐	☐	☐
I am happy with my training on this	☐	☐	☐	☐	☐

Your confidence on what to do

	1	2	3	4	5
Who to ask about this	☐	☐	☐	☐	☐
Who deals with record enquiries	☐	☐	☐	☐	☐

When would you like your next training on this topic?

- As soon as possible ☐
- In 1 month ☐
- In 3 months ☐
- In 6 months ☐
- In 12 months ☐

Your notes

6.29- Information & Data Security

ABSTRACT
1. We must protect confidential information
2. Be careful when sending and receiving information
3. If in doubt, always talk to someone who knows the rules

POLICY
All personal information about Service Users and your co-workers is confidential.
Most important is information about treatment and medical conditions.
Mishandling this can result in prosecution and disciplinary action.

Who is responsible
- Each of us is responsible for taking care about how we send and receive information
- Be sure about the identity of who you are sending to
- If in doubt, always refer to the person responsible for information governance

Things you should know
- Make sure you have received training and ask if you are unsure
- Take care when sending and receiving the Service User's records.
- What is the best way to send and receive sensitive information

What your manager has to do
- Know the rules on Service Users' consent before sending information to others
- When they can refuse to disclose information
- Make sure that staff understand about access to records
- Make sure that Service Users know about access to their records.

Rate your achievement

Your level of confidence

How do you rate yourself?

1	2	3	4	5

I understand this policy ☐ ☐ ☐ ☐ ☐
I understand our procedures ☐ ☐ ☐ ☐ ☐
I am happy with my training on this ☐ ☐ ☐ ☐ ☐

Your confidence on what to do

Who you can ask about this ☐ ☐ ☐ ☐ ☐
Who you should report problems to ☐ ☐ ☐ ☐ ☐

When would you like your next training on this topic?

As soon as possible ☐
In 1 month ☐
In 3 months ☐
In 6 months ☐
In 12 months ☐

Your notes

6.30 - Confidentiality

ABSTRACT
1. All Service User information should be treated as confidential
2. Do not disclose unless you are familiar with the rules
3. Refer disclosure requests to someone who is trained and authorised to do so

POLICY
Service Users have the right to privacy and confidentiality and to expect their confidential information be kept safe and secure. We have both a professional and legal duty to keep information they provide to be kept confidential and to respect their privacy.

Adapted from NHS Constitution Handbook [page 59]

Maintaining confidentiality is an obligation for all staff.
What we should do:
- Person-identifiable or confidential information must be handled with care
- Prevent improper disclosure when information is received, stored, transmitted or disposed of.
- Information is to be processed on a need-to-know basis.
- Always keep a record of what was disclosed and why it was disclosed.
- Only disclose what is absolutely necessary.

Any breach of these rules can result in Disciplinary Action:-
- Breach of confidentiality
- Inappropriate use of data, staff records or business sensitive/confidential information.
- Abuse of computer systems
- Disciplinary offences can result in dismissal

Rate your achievement

Your level of confidence

How do you rate yourself?

| 1 | 2 | 3 | 4 | 5 |

I understand this policy ☐ ☐ ☐ ☐ ☐
I understand our procedures ☐ ☐ ☐ ☐ ☐
I am happy with my training on this ☐ ☐ ☐ ☐ ☐

Your confidence on what to do

Someone asks for private information ☐ ☐ ☐ ☐ ☐
What information you can give out ☐ ☐ ☐ ☐ ☐
Who to ask if you're in doubt ☐ ☐ ☐ ☐ ☐

When would you like your next training on this topic?

As soon as possible ☐
In 1 month ☐
In 3 months ☐
In 6 months ☐
In 12 months ☐

Your notes

6.31- Incidents & Significant Events

ABSTRACT
1. Record every incident and report this to the manager
2. Resolve minor incidents if you can
3. Refer these to the Responsible Officer in a timely manner, especially urgent or serious ones

POLICY
We are required to record and manage all accidents, incidents and near misses which, either caused, or could have caused, injury or death to individuals or damage or loss.

How we deal with these as a team:
- Review what happened, whether a near miss or actual incident
- Analyse the impact, injury or damage from this incident
- Understand how it happened and the cause
- Look at what action was taken or should be taken to manage this at the time

Prevention measures we look at
- Is this likely to happen again?
- How could this have been minimised?
- What measures can we put in place to avoid recurrence?
- What lessons can be learnt from this?
- Discuss at team meetings so everyone knows better

What you should do
- Record and report any incidents you observe
- Resolve minor issues if you can
- Make sure the Service User is safe
- Take immediate action if it is urgent or serious
- Always report this to your manager

Rate your achievement

Your level of confidence

How do you rate yourself?

	1	2	3	4	5
I understand this policy	☐	☐	☐	☐	☐
I understand our procedures	☐	☐	☐	☐	☐
I am happy with my training on this	☐	☐	☐	☐	☐

Your confidence on what to do

	1	2	3	4	5
How to record and report an incident	☐	☐	☐	☐	☐
What to do with serious issues	☐	☐	☐	☐	☐

When would you like your next training on this topic?

- As soon as possible ☐
- In 1 month ☐
- In 3 months ☐
- In 6 months ☐
- In 12 months ☐

Your notes

6.32- Best Practice, Guidance, Alerts

ABSTRACT
1. Always follow best practice and national guidance.
2. We should act on it, not just read it and file it.
3. Be ready to report it if you see this is not being done

POLICY
We should always follow best practice and official guidance.
Just reading our rules and guidelines is just the first step. The most important thing is to actually follow this as you work.

Where does this come from
- Government organisations, and professional bodies
- From people sharing experiences about what works well
- From professional bodies if you belong to one

Best practice
Check whether you are following best practice as you do the task.
Be ready to learn, improve and find better ways of doing things.
Make suggestions and share what you learn with others.

Types of Safety Alerts:-
Medicines alerts: For warnings about the effects of medicines
Medical Devices alerts: For devices found to be faulty or dangerous
Patient Safety alerts: Clinical Alerts and Clinical Guidance

What you should know:-
- What to do if you are sent an alert
- What to do if you see a breach of rules
- What to do if there is potential harm to Service Users
- Who is responsible for keeping staff informed about guidance and alerts

Rate your achievement

Your level of confidence

How do you rate yourself?

	1	2	3	4	5
I understand this policy	☐	☐	☐	☐	☐
I understand our procedures	☐	☐	☐	☐	☐
I am happy with my training on this	☐	☐	☐	☐	☐

Your confidence on what to do

	1	2	3	4	5
Keeping up to date with best practice	☐	☐	☐	☐	☐
Who to ask about this	☐	☐	☐	☐	☐
How to suggest improvements	☐	☐	☐	☐	☐

When would you like your next training on this topic?

- As soon as possible ☐
- In 1 month ☐
- In 3 months ☐
- In 6 months ☐
- In 12 months ☐

Your notes

6.33 - Complaints

ABSTRACT
1. Deal with complaints promptly and follow our set procedures
2. Managers must be told immediately
3. Treat Service Users with respect and dignity

POLICY
- You should know what to do when a complaint is made.
- A complaint can be verbal, electronic or in writing
- It can also be made by the Service User's family or a representative acting on their behalf

When a complaint is received:
- Record the complaint at the earliest opportunity
- Inform your Line Manager or designated person immediately
- Resolve minor issues on the spot if possible
- Take urgent action if it is or looks serious

Help the person with making the complaint
- Make them feel they can complain without fear
- Treat them with courtesy, dignity, respect and compassion
- Be fair and do not discriminate against any user because of their age, ethnicity, religion, gender or disability.
- Make sure they know our procedure for filing complaints
- Assure them that the service is not affected by the complaint
- Be aware they have the capacity for decisions and consent
- Involve the person's representative where appropriate

What we must achieve as a team:
- Deal with complaints quickly and in a timely manner
- Share your experience and suggestions for improvement
- Aim to put things right and prevent this happening again.
- Listen and learn from the experience

Rate your achievement

Your level of confidence

How do you rate yourself?

	1	2	3	4	5
I understand this policy	☐	☐	☐	☐	☐
I understand our procedures	☐	☐	☐	☐	☐
I am happy with my training on this	☐	☐	☐	☐	☐

Your confidence on what to do

	1	2	3	4	5
They don't know how to file a complaint	☐	☐	☐	☐	☐
It is a serious complaint	☐	☐	☐	☐	☐
The person can't speak English	☐	☐	☐	☐	☐

When would you like your next training on this topic?

- As soon as possible ☐
- In 1 month ☐
- In 3 months ☐
- In 6 months ☐
- In 12 months ☐

Your notes

6.34 - Continuous Improvement

ABSTRACT
1. We want to improve on things we are already good at
2. We want to improve where things are not quite right
3. We want to improve on our quality of care, our service and our staff

POLICY
Service Users have the right to expect us to monitor and make efforts to continuously improve the quality of their care. This includes improvements to the safety, effectiveness and experience of services.

Adapted from NHS Constriction Handbook [page 43 & page 44]

What we aim to do
- Observe how we all work and improve where we can
- Learn from our mistakes
- Learn from our achievements and repeat what works well
- Learn from examples of others and best practice

Why we do this
- So we can provide a better service
- So we can provide a safer service
- Our staff get better
- Our operations run smoother and stress free
- Service Users respect and appreciate our professionalism
- We want to be the best we can at our jobs

Rate your achievement

Your level of confidence

How do you rate yourself?

1	2	3	4	5

I understand this policy ☐ ☐ ☐ ☐ ☐
I understand our procedures ☐ ☐ ☐ ☐ ☐
I am happy with my training on this ☐ ☐ ☐ ☐ ☐

Your confidence on what to do

How do you make improvements? ☐ ☐ ☐ ☐ ☐
How to make suggestions ☐ ☐ ☐ ☐ ☐
☐ ☐ ☐ ☐ ☐

When would you like your next training on this topic?

As soon as possible ☐
In 1 month ☐
In 3 months ☐
In 6 months ☐
In 12 months ☐

Your notes

Policies - Things I need help on

Date / Page	Note of what you need help on (Tick as 'Done' when you've got the help)	Done
		☐
		☐
		☐
		☐
		☐
		☐
		☐
		☐

Speak to your manager or supervisor to get help on the topic

7- Full index

1- HOW TO USE THIS BOOK 1

1.1- It's your personal Passport 2
1.2- Getting Started 3
1.3- You Can Write in This Book 4
1.1- Being Professional 4
1.4- Rate Your Confidence on Topics 5
1.5- Different Ways of Working 6
1.6- You can take it anywhere 7
1.7- What if ? 8
1.8- First Time Use 9

2- MY PORTFOLIO 11

2.2- My Positive Experiences 12
2.3- My Suggestions for Improvement 13
2.4- Staff Training Record 14
2.5- Staff Training Record 15
2.6- External Courses and Online Training 16

3- PERSONAL DEVELOPMENT 19

3.1- About Me 20
3.2- Working with Others 21
3.3- Approach to Work 22
3.4- Office Admin – Records and Filing 23
3.5- Office Admin – communications 24
3.6- Organisation Skills 25
3.7- Healthcare Office Skills 26

4- REGULATIONS AND SAFE CARE 29

- 4.2- CQC – 5 Key Domains 30
- 4.3- Terminology you should know 31

5- KNOWLEDGE & TRAINING 37

- 5.2- Being Professional 38
- 5.3- Recognising Risk 39
- 5.4- Treating People with Care 40
- 5.5- Choice and Preferences 41
- 5.6- Informed Consent 42
- 5.7- Sharing information 43
- 5.8- Service User safety 44
- 5.9- Incident Management 45
- 5.10- Medicines Management 46
- 5.11- Care Standards 47
- 5.12- Prescriptions 48
- 5.13- Safeguarding 49
- 5.14- Abuse 50
- 5.15- Vulnerable Persons 51
- 5.16- When things go wrong 52
- 5.17- Complaints 53
- 5.18- Emergencies & Serious incidents 54
- 5.19- Health & Safety 55
- 5.20- Safe Premises & Equipment 56
- 5.21- Fire Safety 57
- 5.22- Clinical Safety 58
- 5.23- Your Personal Welfare 59
- 5.24- Your Personal Safety 60
- 5.25- Cleanliness 61
- 5.26- Clean Premises and Equipment 62
- 5.27- Hand hygiene 63
- 5.28- Infection control 64

5.29- Confidentiality & Caldicott	65
5.30- Confidentiality – Dos and Don'ts	66
5.31- Records	67
5.32- Data Protection	68
5.33- Equality and Diversity	69
5.34- Discrimination	70
6- POLICIES	**73**
6.2- Service Users	74
6.3- Appropriate Care	76
6.4- Access to Care	78
6.5- Collaborative Care	80
6.6- Workplace Safety	82
6.7- Infection Control	84
6.8- Medicines and Controlled Drugs	86
6.9- Fire Safety	88
6.10- Recruitment Policy	90
6.11- Equal Opportunities	92
6.12- Staff Sufficiency & Suitability	94
6.13- Professional Development	96
6.14- Bullying and Harassment	98
6.15- Whistleblowing	100
6.16- Disciplinary and Grievance	102
6.17- Care and Planning	104
6.18- Duty of Candour & Openness	106
6.19- Intimate, Physical Care & Chaperone	108
6.20- Health, Nutrition & Wellbeing	110
6.21- Safeguarding	112
6.22- Managing Mental Health & Disability	114
6.23- Prescriptions Management	116
6.24- Informed Consent	118

- 6.25 - INVOLVEMENT IN CARE 120
- 6.26 - PROVISION OF LIFESTYLE 122
- 6.27 - DIGNITY & RESPECT 124
- 6.28 - ACCESS TO RECORDS 126
- 6.29 - INFORMATION & DATA SECURITY 128
- 6.30 - CONFIDENTIALITY 130
- 6.31 - INCIDENTS & SIGNIFICANT EVENTS 132
- 6.32 - BEST PRACTICE, GUIDANCE, ALERTS 134
- 6.33 - COMPLAINTS 136
- 6.34 - CONTINUOUS IMPROVEMENT 138

7 - FULL INDEX 141

8 - ANNUAL DECLARATION 145

8- Annual Declaration

Your level of confidence

How do you rate yourself?

| 1 | 2 | 3 | 4 | 5 |

1. How to use this book
2. My portfolio
3. Personal development
4. Regulations and safe care
5. Knowledge & training record
6. Policies

What can we do better

Rate the importance

| 1 | 2 | 3 | 4 | 5 |

More help on topics
More discussions with line manager
More staff meetings
Help improve skills and training

Signed by staff	Signed by manager

© everythingCQC.com All rights reserved
Produced by everythingCQC.com under licence from X-Genics
Limited and MaDiHC Limited

All rights reserved. No part of this publication may be reproduced, distributed, or transmitted in any form or by any means, including photocopying, recording, or other electronic or mechanical methods, without the prior written permission of the publisher, except in the case of brief quotations embodied in critical reviews and certain other non-commercial uses permitted by copyright law.

For permission requests write to:
X-Genics Limited, Linden House, Court Lodge Farm, Warren Road, Chelsfield, Kent BR6 6ER

Printed in Great Britain
by Amazon